NO BUGLES FOR SPIES

Tales of the OSS

by

ROBERT HAYDEN ALCORN

D1292269

DAVID McKAY CO., INC.

New York

NO BUGLES FOR SPIES: TALES OF THE OSS

COPYRIGHT © 1962 BY ROBERT HAYDEN ALCORN

LIBRARY OF CONGRESS CATALOG CARD NUMBER: 62-20230

MANUFACTURED IN THE UNITED STATES OF AMERICA

VAN REES PRESS • NEW YORK

FOREWORD

IT SEEMS incredible that thirty thousand people could keep a secret. It is the more unbelievable when one realizes that those thirty thousand persons were scattered throughout the world. They represented every nationality, every type of individual, every religion, every political belief, every economic condition. Yet such was the vast complex of the Office of Strategic Services, the OSS of the war years, the first independent, autonomous and all-encompassing espionage and sabotage agency ever sponsored by the United States Government. The very fact that still, after twenty years, little is known of its work or function is a tribute to its competence.

We live in an age of publicity, of public relations and the public image when even our churches have public relations staffs to "tell all." As a people we consider it important to be known, to let the public in on our activities. It is the more remarkable, therefore, that we as a nation were able to submerge this tendency for exposure long enough to accomplish the clandestine work of an organization like the OSS. But that we did points up the high discipline of the people who made up that organization.

Its members withstood and, to some degree, welcomed the snide quips that were considered "bright" cocktail chatter in Washington in the early days of the war. Oh So Social. Oh So

Secret. Oh Such Snobs. The variety was endless but at least it divulged nothing of the real OSS. Then, as the agency grew and began to function actively in the war theaters, there was an amusing confusion that continually appeared. Whenever any passing reference was made to OSS, more often than not, the non-OSS listener assumed that the reference was to SOS, the Army's supply services. We were aways happy to let the misunderstanding pass uncorrected. It was just one more way of protecting the security of the organization.

There are no bugles for spies. Nor are there banners and bands for saboteurs. They have no morale-bracing buddies to spur them on when the going is the toughest. They have no vast housekeeping mechanism behind them in the field to see that they are properly fed, adequately sheltered and medically tended. They are alone. They are alone in every way, alone in their work, alone in their very livelihood, alone especially in their thoughts, dependent on their own resources as they have never been before in their lives. They must be wary of every contact, guarded of every word, cautious in every movement. And as if that were not enough there are the problems of everyday living, how they are to eat, where they are to sleep and how they shall work. It is all up to them alone.

Then, when the most terrifying of all possibilities becomes reality, when one is captured, the spy is irretrievably, cruelly alone. Then his very existence is ignored. Those closest to him desert and deny him. The organization for which he works has never heard of him. He lives with tortures, or he dies, alone. And often his death is just a vanishing, his actual passing unknown, his grave unmarked.

All this he knows beforehand and he accepts it as he accepts the fact that he is expendable. The mission, the network, all the undercover operation of the silent colossus for which he works must be protected so that it may go on even at the sacrifice of his own life.

Ruthless? Cold-blooded? Sinister? Espionage is all of these

things and more. It is also very brave. For it is one thing to go into battle with hundreds of others when all hell has let loose and a kind of hysteria carries you forward. It is quite another thing to drop silently into the very midst of the enemy with, really, only your wits to save you. Wits and a colossal amount of steel-nerved courage.

The OSS recruited, trained and operated countless individuals of rare courage and resourcefulness. Many went into enemy territory not once, but several times, and lived to slip quietly back into the everyday world of peace. Some served with high distinction only to end in a twilight zone of insanity. Some never came back.

This then is their story. This is how it was. It cannot possibly be *about* them all, they were too numerous for that, but it is *of* them all, for they all had one thing in common: the ultimate in courage. Only the details, only the locale, only the specific mission would be the variable.

All of these stories are true. They may be incredible, they may be horrible, they may be fantastic or amusing but they are true and they are related as they happened. Only the names and other details pertinent to security have been altered.

There are many that can never be told and that is, perhaps, just as well. But what has been attempted here is no exposé, no "how to" book on espionage. It is quite simply the story of OSS, what it was, how it grew, what it did. Actually *how* it operated is not here. But the story of some of its people is here.

That is the important thing.

Suffield, Connecticut.
May 8, 1962.

CONTENTS

NO BUGLES FOR SPIES

Tales of the OSS

CHAPTER 1

DUVAL

OF COURSE no one knows for certain what makes a good agent and unless you are able to look on the whole business of espionage and sabotage as a tremendous gamble you shouldn't be involved in it. At best you can only lay down a few basic qualities of character to look for and then tell yourself that no one can assure you that any given agent really has them. Nerve? Certainly. But what passes for nerve under even the most rigorous training may turn into a devastating blue funk when the chips are down and the agent finds himself on his own among enemies. Patriotism and loyalty? Of course. But who is to say that these will not fade under torture and turn the most steadfast operative into the most dreaded of all espionage weapons, the double agent? Intelligence? Without it your man is dead for, once in enemy territory and on his own completely, his every motion, his every act must be considered and "forethought" in a way he had never previously conceived. The British once uncovered a double agent in Egypt because he forgot to urinate in the approved fashion of the native men, with the knees slightly bent. And as Americans operating on the continent one of the first things we had to teach our operatives was how to "eat continental" without shifting the knife and fork from hand to hand with each mouthful of food.

So you gamble. You look over the files on the various volunteers—it's operational suicide to think you can mount an operation with draft personnel—study the qualifications and background, pick a man and plunge.

I must say that Duval looked the most unlikely prospect in the flesh. His file was excellent. He was twenty-six, five feet eight and one hundred and forty-eight pounds. He was the son of a prominent American father and a French mother, had lived eighteen years of his life in France, been educated there and, of course, spoke the language like a native. And I can remember his saying to me the first time we talked that he had two strong loyalties in his life, to America and to France, and for that reason he was volunteering for action in any manner we thought might be helpful to the Allied cause.

Perhaps because I myself hadn't been in the game too long, I had expected more bluster, more aggressiveness in a prospective agent. Duval had none of that. He was quiet, almost shy, and his voice was modulated to the point of being colorless. Physically his body was wiry and well muscled, the result of much swimming, riding and tennis, but there was a fineness about the features, a quality to the bone structure which seemed to say too much gentleness was there to be really tough, really able to take it.

Other factors outweighed these apparent flaws. His family

2

owned a country place not far from one of the large rail centers in occupied France and he knew the area intimately. We set up a plan for him.

Duval went into uniform as a private and was sent off for his basic training. Through arrangements with the Army, the Office of Strategic Services saved itself much time and organizational problems by having such personnel trained and conditioned in regular Army training areas until they were ready to go into our own specialized schools. This also gave OSS an opportunity to observe our man under rigorous training without in any way exposing him to our super-secret areas. Just in case he proved to be a washout, he could be released without endangering the security of other agents in training.

Duval came out of his basic training tanned, fit and rugged. He was sent to one of our schools, now under an assumed name, the name he would use henceforth in all of his war career, and with an entirely new and fictitious personal background. This had been worked out with him and he had been drilled and re-drilled in the most minute details until his real life seemed no longer to exist. His schoolmates were equally fictitious characters and each and every one of them was instructed to try to "break the cover" of the others. And they all knew that here and now had begun their very struggle for survival, that any slip now could well mean death later in the field. The tension began to mount.

The rigorous physical training went on without letup, but now Duval was spending more hours on those things which would point to his own special mission. He was instructed in the uses of short-wave radio, not only how to operate a set but also how to repair one with only the most makeshift and improbable articles at hand. He was instructed in code. He was taught not only the use of various types of firearms, but how to dismantle them and again, how to repair them by "cannibalizing"—taking parts from other disabled pieces. He learned how to handle explosives, how to blow bridges, derail trains,

3

destroy ammunition dumps and hundreds of related problems.

He learned how to break into closely guarded offices and to microfilm secret documents.

The training for this deserves some description for it shows the intricate cooperation for mutual benefit between different organizations during the war. General Donovan, Chief of OSS, had approached the heads of a few key war industries in the Washington-Baltimore area and had worked out a plan whereby OSS agents would, as part of their final espionage training, attempt to break into these war plants. Once inside —and that was not necessarily the easiest part of the assignment—they would have to pick locks, work safe combinations and microfilm secret documents. Under the Donovan agreement only one or two key men in each plant would know of the arrangement and at OSS only General Donovan and the person actually responsible for the agent-trainee would be aware of the plan. In this way our agents were trained under the most realistic conditions. They ran the definite hazard of being shot by a company guard while gaining entry to a plant and yet, once inside, if caught, a code number by phone quickly identified the agent as on a training mission.

From the standpoint of the industries involved, it gave them an excellent way of testing their plant security and of taking steps to plug any holes in it. And though most of them boasted of their security, General Donovan caused some chagrin when, on more than one occasion, he was able to present the head of an industry engaged in the most secret of war work with microfilms of that industry's most guarded papers. He even caused a full scale shake-up in one company when he revealed that one of our agents had succeeded in obtaining employment and then, over a period of weeks, had filmed documents, stolen plans and forged security passes without detection. It was only after OSS felt that the trainee had learned enough that he was withdrawn and the story was told.

Duval went through all of this. And all the while he was

4

being assessed by expert observers, seeking a weakness somewhere. He was pulled and twisted, angered and frustrated, mentally tortured and physically exhausted by a drumming, drumming, drumming routine aimed at making him break, somewhere, anywhere, but break. He was denied sleep until he seemed drunk with exhaustion and then presented with a problem calling for instant alertness and caution. He was held in isolation, a living limbo, in order to weaken him with boredom and then projected into a situation calling for the greatest physical exertion. Through it all Duval showed a quiet calm which delighted his trainers and mystified many others. And all the while he was toughening, mentally, physically and morally toughening against the day when all of this would be real, "for keeps."

I took Duval overseas. We went in a jammed troopship and he looked like all the other thousands of GIs except that he looked more shy, more sensitive and softer than some. It gave me the most tremendous amusement and satisfaction to see how completely he melted into the khaki horde, realizing how much he differed from all the others in resources, toughness and skill under that bland exterior. I often wondered if he saw the contrast.

But now the last touches of his training were to begin. Within twenty-four hours of his arrival in England Duval was at an OSS training area and the real beginning of his mission.

While Duval himself had been undergoing the rigorous preliminary training the details of his mission were being shaped by OSS-London. Our intelligence from occupied France indicated that the area around Lyons was well salted with potential resistance fighters. They had spirit and morale but they lacked direction and arms. Duval was the man to give the direction and through whom we would supply the arms, although I at times found myself wondering if we were not, in the most trite of all expressions, "sending a boy to do a man's job" literally.

5

And just in case Duval himself should have any illusions about the seriousness of his mission, he was now going through even more intensive and grim instruction. He was to live on roots, dried leaves and berries. He was memorizing codes that would tip us off if, captured, he was sending messages under direction from the enemy. He was memorizing safe addresses where he could seek refuge should he need to disappear for a while. And he was learning to kill. Not in the blazing, bloody, screaming manner of sudden assault, but in the silent, bloodless, calculating manner of stealth.

His "cover" was now building up and all of the myriad details necessary to authenticating that "cover" were being gathered. Duval was to go in as a French peasant, clad in the inevitable faded and patched blue workclothes of the type. Everything, underwear, socks, sabots, beret, sweater, jackets and trousers were correct, turned out by OSS' own workrooms where we could produce anything from a ticket stub for a given Paris cinema to ersatz cigarettes, bus timetables, ration and identity cards and spectacles.

By the time he was ready to go a listing of the items to go with him read like the inventory for a one-man invasion from Mars. Radio, of course, to send and receive messages. Arms. For his own use and for the preliminary supply of those first resistance fighters whom he would contact. Ammunition. Flashlights. Emergency food rations. Spirits. Medical kit. Rope. Knife. And money.

Money, as usual was a problem. Enough to do his job and yet not so much as to make him suspect if caught. That was solved by supplying him with wonderfully torn and dirty franc notes of small denominations such as a peasant might carry. Some of these would go in his pockets and socks, the rest to be packaged in waterproof containers so that they might be buried. And with the serial numbers carefully checked at the last moment to assure the money would be safe to use, not caught up in one of the Germans' sudden invalidating orders declaring a certain series worthless.

Now he was ready. All the tedious, straining weeks and months of preparation pointing to this one operation were being brought together like the threads of some vast loom. Dozens of faceless unknowns had worked on segments of this project. They had worked without really knowing what they were working on or for whom and here was this boy, Duval, at the center, completely at the mercy of the training, the planning, the resourcefulness and the cunning of men he had never seen, his life in their hands. It is strange that there is not more tension and yet, when the date is set and the night arrives, there is a calm, a controlled efficiency about the final preparations that is almost chilling in retrospect.

They started dressing Duval about nine o'clock. From the skin out every item was given a final appraisal to insure against some telltale giveaway which could tip the enemy to his origins and mission. The excitement mounted as this American GI was transformed before their eyes into a rather dull-looking French peasant. It was so good, so convincing, we hesitated to cover it all up with the crash helmet and the camouflage coverall he would wear for the jump. So they sat for a while in the flight shack and had a cup of coffee with our Frenchman. He was relaxed, the same calm, shy, quiet person I had first interviewed so many months ago.

In the distance now one could hear the roar of the motors as his plane warmed up on the runway. The talk over the coffee quickened slightly, perhaps a trifle nervously, but it remained trivial. Suddenly a sergeant came quickly into the shack, saluted, and announced that the pilot was ready whenever we were. We checked over again, and for the last time, the equipment which was already loaded on the plane to be dropped with Duval.

The airfield was black and only the motors glowed to show us where the plane stood on the ramp. Then, as one's eyes ad-

7

justed to the dark, one could see the soft dull yellow of the lighted interior of the plane. They walked quickly to the ramp in the chill wind, thinking of all the things it was now too late to say, Duval striding along laden with parachute and equipment. At the foot of the ramp he turned and held out his hand.

"Thank you, sir, for all you have done. I hope I won't let you down." He sounded almost diffident.

An officer squeezed his hand and grasped him by one shoulder.

"You can't miss. Good luck."

He went up the ramp followed by the sergeant and in a moment the door closed. There was a tremendous roar as the motors revved, the plane swung out into the darkness and taxied away. For a while one could make out its receding outline in the blacked-out field and then it became only a diminishing sound. Then, there was a lull, a crash of sound growing louder, louder, louder until it had passed us by and he was airborne.

We turned and went into the flight shack.

It was the dark of the moon.

The phrase really had had little meaning for Duval until now. He had heard it used over and over again, casually, during his training, and he had come to recognize the fact that it was the dark of the moon which we most desired to conceal the implementation of our espionage and sabotage "drops."

But now he knew.

The inside of the huge bomber was in darkness, the black pierced only by tiny electric eyes which glowed either red, yellow or green. The red was glowing now which meant that they were still off target. He watched it with a kind of stupefaction, hypnotized by its small steady gleam. It was freezing cold in the plane and he huddled uncomfortably on the metal floor. It was impossible to settle into a position of any comfort, laden

8

as he was with parachute, duffel kit, tommy gun, knife and rope.

The steady throb of the motors drilled into him until now there was a rhythm within the rhythm of sound, numbing and deadening. He tried to fight the numbing conspiracy of cold and throb by shifting his weight, hugging himself closer and then mentally going over his equipment. Almost by rote he could check off the clothing—heavy long underwear, heavy sweater and the faded blue denim trousers and jacket of the French peasant. He had stuffed the soft beret into his pocket and was wearing a jump helmet. This, and a kind of smock made of brown, black and green camouflage material, would be discarded as soon as he hit the ground.

There was a tap on his shoulder and he looked up. The sergeant was standing over him and offering a cup of hot chocolate. He took the cup clumsily with his mittened fingers, yelled his thanks above the roar of the motors and smiled at the sergeant. The chocolate burned all the way down and he sipped it slowly to make it last. The sergeant sat beside him drinking from his own cup and they tried to make small talk but it was no use. They had to yell and somehow the only things Duval could think of to say seemed silly and too unimportant to yell. So they sat there uncomfortably surrounded by dark and cold and noise and drank their chocolate.

Suddenly the red light vanished and beside the spot where it had shone there glowed a small yellow bulb. Although they had not consciously been watching they both saw it the moment the color changed.

"This is the 'ready.' "

The sergeant tossed the last swallow of chocolate down his throat, crumpled the cup in his hand and went forward in the plane.

A sudden prickly, hot-cold tingling flowed through Duval's body, the numbing sensation of cold and noise seemed to vanish and he struggled to his feet. He finished the chocolate

9

standing in the plane, his feet braced against the slight tilt of the flooring.

"We'll be over your target area in about ten minutes."

The sergeant had come back from the cockpit and began readying for the drop. He tested the static line which was to trip the parachute open. He released the catches which held the cover over the "joe hole," the trap in the plane's floor through which Duval was to jump. Duval watched his preparations while he himself checked for the hundredth time his parachute, his kit, his gun, his knife.

The sergeant was working methodically now and efficiently. He went once more to the front of the plane, spoke into the intercom, listened, nodded and then, looking over at Duval, pointed up to the little light panel.

The yellow light blinked out and the green came on, blue-green and glaring, in the darkness. The plane now was banking and circling, the motors were cut and it was almost silent in the cabin. Duval could feel the loss of altitude in his ears.

"We're running in now. We're almost on target. We'll circle once and when he levels off, jump."

Duval heard it all and nodded.

The sergeant had flipped the cover from the "joe hole," hooked the static line in place and motioned Duval to the hole.

Duval inched forward, slid on the floor of the plane and glanced through the hole. All was blackness, not so black as the interior of the plane, but black nonetheless and he could, he thought, see the flicker of a pinpoint of light. The air was rushing into the plane through the hole and it was all he could do to force his legs down and out until they were hanging through. The wind tore at them and he gripped the sides of the hole with all his strength.

Gradually he could feel the plane levelling off and there was hardly the sound of a motor as the pilot went into a glide. The sergeant was facing him across the hole, watching him intently and speaking encouragement with his eyes.

10

"Ready? We're running in."

Duval nodded. His body tensed.

The sergeant leaned across to him and, above the wild whistling of the wind, yelled, "Good luck. Clean the bastards out and I'll see you in Berlin. JUMP!"

The last word was like an electric shock. Duval shoved forward and down on his arms, shot through the hole and was out of the plane. He went straight and felt the fresh bite of the cold air rushing past him, heard the receding roar of the plane as it swung away and gained altitude and felt the tug on his harness as the parachute opened.

Quite suddenly everything seemed unreal. After the din and throb of the plane, after the tension and the excitement of waiting for this moment, he found himself floating in dark silence over blacked-out French countryside and he almost felt relaxed. Somewhere below him was his target area and, supposedly, a couple of friendly French resistance fighters waiting for him.

He peered down into the black and then he saw them. Winking, on, off, on, off, like tiny stars, Duval made out the sharp shafts of light. It pleased and amazed him to realize that he was almost directly on target and he almost spoke aloud his gratitude to the pilot. The lights were placed and winking just as London had said they would be: four lights marking each corner of a rectangle and a fifth glowing from dead center. He was able to judge the speed of his descent roughly by the rate at which the lights seemed to spread apart below him.

Then, almost without warning, he was on the ground. What had seemed a slow drifting descent suddenly changed; he saw the dark earth rushing toward him and there he was rolling over and over and struggling to control his chute lines as he skidded and bumped across the soft plough. He unbuckled his harness as he rose to his feet, gathered his parachute, ripped off his crash helmet and camouflage smock and rolled them into a bundle. The next moment he was on his knees digging

11

in the soft earth with his bare hands and burying his parachute equipment. The soil seemed light and moist and he wondered if London had worked this out for him as well, earth soft enough to be dug with the hands.

When he had finished he sat back on his haunches to get his breath. There was a stillness over the field and he looked about him in the dark. As far as he could make out he was in a large field, no trees, no buildings and then, as his eyes searched the darkness, he thought he could make out a line of trees in the distance. But now there were no lights and no sound. It was as if he were abandoned in a shadowed world. He wanted desperately to light a cigarette and yet he knew that could be a fatal act. Somewhere, in that field or along its borders, eyes were searching for him, friendly eyes he was sure, but there could be others.

He rubbed the dirt from his hands, pulled the beret from his pocket and put it on and then drew on his mittens. He looked over the little mound of earth where he had buried his jump gear, threw more dirt on it and then rose to his feet. His next move would be what seemed the hopeless task of finding the two loads of equipment which had been dropped with him.

A soft, staccato whistle just to his left made him drop to the ground. There was a long silence and then the soft whistle again. Duval waited, holding his breath, waiting to be sure. It came a third time and now he was sure. The first two calls had been so soft and so rapid he dared not acknowledge the code. But the third call was the distinct dot, dot, dot, dash of the V signal.

Duval whistled a soft reply, the dot, dot, dot, dash in a higher key. There was a long silence and for one chilling moment he wondered if he had been tricked. Then, so much closer it startled him, the whistle came again.

Duval raised his head and turned in the direction of the whistle, squinting into the shadows and trying to locate a figure somewhere against the slightly lighter background of the night

12

sky. He looked full circle around him and started again before he saw the figure approaching, a shadow, almost shapeless in the dark, but a man.

The figure stopped a few yards from him and whistled again. Duval could almost see the startled reaction of his body when the whistled reply came so near at hand. He paused for a moment and then started forward again. Duval reached quietly for his gun and rose quickly to his feet.

"Monsieur de Londres?"

The voice was subdued, husky.

"Monsieur de Lyons?" Duval still had his hand on his gun as he answered. It wasn't needed.

The figure rushed forward and with all of the exuberance and effusiveness of the French embraced Duval, kissed him on each cheek, hugged him, slapped him on the back and broke into an enthusiastic babble of welcome and enquiry.

I would find it hard to believe that any enemy agent ever arrived in enemy territory with more fanfare than Duval. And I can still see the incredulous look on his face as he told me of the reception that awaited him on his arrival in France. After all, he had been trained for months for a most dangerous and secret mission and he had been keyed to a pitch of alert for his own preservation. He had not been prepared for what followed his first contact with Monsieur de Lyons, whose cover name was Armand.

Talking constantly and with the natural excitement of a host welcoming a long awaited guest, Armand guided Duval from the field. The lights? Ah, yes, there were five men with flashlights to beam straight into the air to mark the target for the pilot and for Duval's descent. But there were others as well. There were spotters assigned to watch for and retrieve the two supply drops released with Duval. They had had no trouble at all; they had found the drops, already buried the chutes and hidden the supplies.

13

Armand explained all of this as he led the way along a furrow of the field. His sabots were heavy with the clinging mud of the ploughed field and at the edge of the field he stopped to scrape some of it off on the turf. Duval cleaned his sabots as well. He decided to let Armand do most of the talking and it was perhaps easier that way for Armand could hardly have been interrupted. Duval could now make out the outline of a wood, huge, looming trees showing the first feathery traces of bursting leaf buds against the dark sky and suddenly, there were several figures approaching under the trees.

Armand made a rather flowery introduction of Monsieur de Londres to the other men and each one came forward with the shy seriousness of the French peasant and shook Duval's hand. There was a moment of general conversation concerning the drops, the hiding of the supplies and the burying of the chutes and then, with all the aplomb of a grand seigneur, Armand led the group through the wood toward a cluster of farm buildings. Duval could almost picture the arrangement without seeing it, the brick and stone barns and sheds, the walled yard and the stone cottage almost a part of the barns, but all dark, tight shut against the night air. All at once he realized how the blackout must have been easy for the French as it was their custom of centuries to bolt and bar and darken everything against the night.

The group was now more subdued as they crossed the enclosed farm-yard and headed for the largest of the farm buildings, a huge brick barn with solid walls and apparently no windows. Armand rapped quickly on the heavy wooden door, waited a moment and rapped again. Duval noted the dot, dot, dot, dash of the V signal. There was a long pause. Then, quietly, slowly, the huge door was opened. A crude curtain of old sacking formed a sort of vestibule and screened any light from the interior of the building. A young woman, bundled in heavy sweaters and slacks and carrying sidearms, grunted an acknowledgement as Armand slipped past her. She grunted again at Duval as if he were just another of the group and the heavy salutation was repeated for each one as he entered.

The scene before Duval made him think of some grotesque caricature of a cocktail party. The barn was jammed with a motley crowd of men and women, boys and girls, signalled into silence until the door had been closed after the last visitor and now again chattering and laughing, smoking and drinking with all the relaxed unconcern of party-goers. Huge straw torches lighted the scene and gave off a smoke which was supposed to escape through a vent in the roof of the barn but which for the most part seemed to hang in the heavy air. Armand worked his way through the crowd, stopping now and then to introduce Duval to someone and then moving on.

At the far end of the barn a group of men and women were working over a fire pit turning several small pigs on spits and stirring huge smoking black iron kettles of vegetables and broths. They had set up plank tables on sawhorses along the sides of the room and there were the inevitable bottles of red wine ranged down the center of the tables. Armand spoke a few words with one of the women who seemed to be in charge of the cooking, turned, and climbed up onto one of the plank tables.

"*Mes amis.*" His voice boomed above the din of the room and Duval was impressed with the immediate silence and attention which greeted his salutation. "Monsieur de Londres is now with us."

There was an instant, exultant cheer, at first a garbled roar of approval and then distinguishable *Vives, Vive la France, Vive l'Angleterre, Vivent les Etats Unis.* Duval felt emotion rise within him. But he was uneasy.

As Armand went on with his short speech, a sort of pep talk at once extolling Duval and the Allies and cursing the Boches, Duval stood quietly to one side assessing the situation. He had been trained for months for this assignment. He had been impressed with the need for caution, for absolute secrecy, for

15

anonymity. He had jumped into occupied France expecting to make contact with Armand and perhaps one or two others and then hiding out for a few days just in case his "drop" had been spotted by any German garrisons in the neighborhood. And now here he was, less than an hour after landing, catapulted into the midst of a full scale celebration of his arrival. It was hardly a situation to put an agent at ease.

He made his plans during the meal. As soon as Armand had finished his speech he had tried to get Duval to mount the table beside him and say a few words. Duval was able to avoid such a conspicuous show and got off with a few trite phrases from the floor and a plea for everyone to get on with the feasting. It worked.

The meal was good and abundant and it made him at last aware of his hunger. And while they ate he talked quietly with Armand of his next moves. He would, when the after dinner drinking began in earnest, slip unnoticed out of the barn and leave the area for at least three days. During that time Armand could check over the supplies that had been cached, decide what four men he would pick for the first cadre of trainees and be ready to begin operations when Duval returned. One other was let in on the plan, a slight youth of Duval's general physical appearance, who was to act as a stand-in just in case the drinkers got out of hand and called for toasts and a speech from Monsieur de Londres.

It was past three o'clock in the morning when Duval finally grunted his way past the girl at the barn door. It amused him to think that at one point he had worried lest his leaving would be noticed. The party was now a raucous, drunken brawl. There were groups of ribald storytellers, groups of singers, isolated twosomes making love and many more just sleeping. The crisp, still freshness of the air came as a tremendous stimulant and he walked rapidly down the farm road, following Armand's directions as if he had travelled the area many times before.

16

Then, as the pre-dawn light greyed the fields, he began to recognize certain landmarks. It had been four years, almost five, since he had been here and yet these very woods and fields were as familiar to him as if he had left them only a few days ago. A sudden, consuming wave of nostalgia flowed through him and he paused by a large tree and looked out over the soft unevenness of the fields. Little puffs of cottony mist hung in the low pockets and the tufts of woodland seemed wrapped in grey gauze. There, to the right, was the large wood with the manicured allées through which he had so often galloped his pony as a child and off to the left was the huge field of sugar beets which was low-lying and always muddy, deep going for a pony. An almost audible gasp of emotion broke from his lips as Duval realized that his family's place lay hidden in the mists of distance not four miles away, now taken over by the Germans as some sort of billet or staff headquarters. It seemed incredible, in the soft, lazy stillness of the morning, that this was war, that there was war here, all around him, quiet, sinister, treacherous war apparently unrelated to the noisy slaughter of front line slugging.

"Don't go near your family's place, ever," he had been cautioned in London. "You'll be tempted, out of curiosity, but don't. Curiosity kills more agents than carelessness."

The words seemed almost audible to him now as he stood there under the tree, looking across the fields and listening to the first tentative insect and bird sounds of the morning. Without hesitation he took his gun, wrapped it carefully in oiled cloth and buried it under the tree along with the rope which he still had with him. A knife he could retain without too much danger, should he be stopped and searched. And then, just to play safe, he buried some of his surplus francs in a second cache. He cut a deep gash in the spreading root of the tree, rubbed the freshness away with dirt, threw a few leaves over the little graves and walked away.

17

It was morning chore time by the time he had reached the little village and people were now appearing in the streets. Duval, a cigarette with a long ash hanging limply from his lips, went directly to the railway station and bought a ticket for Lyons. This, he figured, would get him out of the area for a few days and also give him the confidence necessary to his free movement about the countryside. Only as he sank back in the railway carriage and closed his eyes did he realize how exhausted and sleepy he really was.

"RAUS! AUFSTEHEN!"

The guttural roar nearly lifted him to his feet. Standing over him in the railway compartment was a tall, hard-faced German in shining black boots, grey uniform and peaked cap of an officer. In the aisle, outside of the compartment, two other Germans were waiting. Two other French peasants who had been sharing the compartment with him were already shrugging their way out into the aisle to the accompaniment of more guttural shouting and much prodding. Duval shook himself, rose and shuffled from the compartment, his heart beating so fast and hard he was sure it could be seen through his smock. The two German officers in the aisle pushed roughly past him, joined the third in the compartment and closed the door. It had all happened so quickly Duval had not had time to panic but he was reassured by the sullen comments of his French travelling companions about the way the Germans appropriated all the best seats to themselves.

There were many German soldiers on the train, too many for comfort, and Duval was relieved when they finally reached Lyons and he was able to lose himself in the crowds. He decided to wander and window-shop in an effort to regain his composure. After all, the shock of seeing his first Germans had taken its toll and he was inwardly nervous, feeling that his every move was being watched, that he was suspect from every angle.

18

A small tobacco shop caught his eye and he went inside. A large, middle-aged Frenchwoman in the usual black dress covered by a heavy grey sweater answered the tinkle of the bell which rang as he opened the door. Her face was flushed as if she had been working over a hot stove and there were the inevitable small gold rings in her pierced ears. Duval bought a pack of ersatz cigarettes and then asked to look at cheap lighters. The woman put a couple on the counter and he fingered them, asked the prices and tried the flint. There was no fluid in them and he asked the price of a can of fluid. The woman filled one of the cheap lighters, flicked it into flame and made a little sale speech. Duval was undecided.

The woman turned to some shelves at her back, rummaged through a few boxes and returned to the counter. Delicately, with thumb and index finger, she placed a gleaming Dunhill lighter in front of Duval. She watched him as he picked it up and her eyes were steadily on him as she spoke.

"This is the best. It was made where Monsieur comes from."

Duval felt the blood rush to the base of his head.

"It would be too expensive," he countered. "I'll take the one you have filled, thank you."

It seemed to take hours for the woman to make change and when she offered to wrap it in cheap paper he said rather brusquely not to bother he would pocket it.

"Merci, Monsieur, et bonne chance." Her voice was light.

Duval was in a trance of semi-panic as he left the shop and went up the street. He dared not walk fast. He dared not look back. He was certain that he would be followed, identified as an agent and captured. It made no difference that the people passing him in the street took no notice of him. Something was the tip-off, but what? Every item of clothing was authentic and safe. It couldn't be that. He spoke French as a second language and he knew the patois of the area.

The street led into a little square with pebble paths, a small statue and benches. Duval dropped onto a bench and reached

19

for a cigarette. His hand was shaking as he lighted it but the first few puffs relaxed and calmed him. The incident in the shop worried and frightened him. He went over and over again, as carefully as possible, every word, every expression he had used in the shop. He could find no clue that should have given him away.

A couple of German soldiers went past and then another group. He was relieved that they seemed not to notice him and he began to enjoy the warming of the morning sun on his back, the busy coming and going of the little square and the contentment of his cigarette after the tension of the morning. More Germans in uniform went by and he was suddenly aware that there seemed to be more Germans passing through the little square than he had noticed proportionately in the streets. He watched one group as it went through the square. They were walking smartly, in formation, and they headed for an imposing building facing him. It could be a municipal building of some kind. His eyes followed them through the square, across the street and up the wide steps of the building until they had disappeared inside. It was then that he saw the sign. Spread across the whole width of the main entrance of the building was a black bordered white rectangle. A huge swastika loomed over it. And printed in bold black letters were the words: *GEHEIME STAATSPOLIZEI*. It was Gestapo headquarters.

That did it. Duval felt his nerve slipping. It was a fatalistic sort of thing, a feeling that he was perhaps pressing his luck just a trifle too far for his own good. He had made a safe landing and contact; he had weathered the hazard of the welcoming celebration; he had not panicked at the first sight of the Germans on the train; he had survived the recognition of his origins by the woman in the tobacco shop; and now he was sitting on a bench not one hundred yards from the front entrance to Gestapo Headquarters for the area.

Without any further assessment of his situation, Duval decided to hide out at a "safe address," one of the havens which awaited him for an emergency. Like every other agent, he had been provided with two or three such hideouts where he could lie up in relative safety while overcoming a case of nerves or eluding pursuit or such related reasons. Any good agent is subject to rattling nerve tension and, if he is a good agent, there is no bravado in trying to override a real case. The good agent recognizes the hazard involved, not only to himself but to all of his accomplices and to the success of his mission, and acts with common sense. That means hiding out until the cause for his nerve tension is removed and he has a grip on himself.

Duval hid out. But on schedule, three days later, he was back with Armand in the country and the real work of his mission began. Armand had picked the four men for the first training cadre and Duval went to work with them. He taught them all he knew about sabotage. He instructed them in the use of the weapons which had been dropped with him. And then, when they could prove their ability, each one of the four was assigned four trainees of his own to instruct.

So it went. With his short-wave code, Duval was in constant contact with London and as his work proceeded and the numbers of resistance workers grew, London dropped more guns, more ammunition, more sabotage supplies for the harassment of the Germans. In retrospect, it seems incredible that there could have been such constant and apparently easy contact with London. It was far from easy. Every message had to be sent with the greatest possible care and never twice from the same location, for the Germans were constantly monitoring the air and zeroing in with direction finders to pinpoint radio contact. To Duval's credit his hideouts were never discovered though there were many close calls.

Six months after his arrival in occupied France, Duval was airlifted back to London for a rest period and further instruction. And then, with more new equipment and a fresh zeal for his job he was dropped again into the area. Four months later

21

we brought him out again for another briefing just prior to D-Day and sent him back with the realization that all of his harrowing months of nerve-cracking work were about to pay off.

And they did. When D-Day finally broke and the Germans began their retreat, Duval's operation alone put nearly seven thousand fully equipped and thoroughly seasoned resistance fighters into the field. They blew German supply dumps, rail lines, bridges. They surprised and decimated German patrols, demoralized the German troops and stimulated the French populace to heroic activity. It meant that when the Allied forces came through the area their action became almost a mop-up of an area already cleared for them by Duval's men.

It was overwhelmingly successful, Duval's mission. And perhaps one reason for its huge success was the fact that early in the operation Duval had decided not to permit any constant, sustained sabotaging of the area. Only occasionally, and sporadically, were the Germans harassed with emery dust in motors, blown supply depots, bridges, rail lines and the like. The result was that the German commandant of the area apparently quite logically believed such sabotage to be the isolated acts of occasional, unorganized saboteurs. At least that is what Duval hoped and it worked. Better, he had argued, to work quietly and relatively unmolested for months and then hit with a real punch than to run the risk of being the object of a concerted hunt as the result of too much early activity.

Duval was awarded the Distinguished Service Cross after the war. He received it with the same diffident, shy and slightly embarrassed calm which seemed to characterize his every act. General Donovan read the citation, added a few warm personal remarks of his own and shook Duval's hand after the medal had been pinned. I found it almost as hard to believe that this man and this heroic record were related, as I had, years previously, found it difficult to visualize him as an effective agent. Which is exactly why he was so good.

Duval? He has his own name and identity back now and he is living abroad. The last time I saw him he still seemed incredibly boyish and very happy with the job he is now doing. But I'm sure that, should you happen to sit next to him at dinner some evening, you might think him a rather colorless, ineffectual character.

CHAPTER 2

THE WIZARD OF OSS

"HE WAS really a very simple person." How many times have we heard it said of the most complex of characters? And how often have we realized that usually the simplicity is more apparent than real, actually the result of refining of temperament, emotions, values, drives, ideas and experience, all the imponderables which go into the formation of a character. In short, it is almost impossible for an intelligent, educated and aggressive leader of men to be simple. He may simplify problems, he may cut to the core of ideas, he may react to situations dynamically but he is not simple in so doing. If anything, such ability only indicates the greater complexity of character. Like the smooth computer box that comes up with instant answers to great problems and thereby makes them seem simple, hiding the complexity of its inner mechanism, so the great "simple" character contains hidden complexities beyond all imagining.

So it was with General Donovan. A man of tremendous physical and mental vigor, aggressive, alert, direct and quick in every way, he might well be referred to as a simple person but he had arrived at that simplicity only by most complex contradictions of character. He was tough and soft. He was hard and gentle. He was dominating and considerate. He was direct and devious. He was a vain ladies' man and he was a rough man's man. He was all of these contradictions but only one side of his character had no opposite. That was his courage. He had courage such as few men ever know. Not the bravado courage of the daredevil but the quiet courage of the man who has no personal fear of anything.

The story of his heroism with the "Fighting 69th" during the First World War needs no retelling. It was spectacular enough to win for him the Congressional Medal of Honor and the nickname "Wild Bill." And as we came up to the Second World War, "Wild Bill" Donovan was one of only three American citizens to hold the three highest decorations bestowed by our country on its heroes: the Congressional Medal of Honor, the Distinguished Service Cross and the Distinguished Service Medal.

I first met General Donovan the day I went on the rolls of the organization that became the Office of Strategic Services. He was Colonel Donovan, then, but in civilian clothes and he was head of a new agency innocuously known as the Office of the Coordinator of Information. It was his own brain child. As he had watched the growing threat of Nazi Germany, "Wild Bill" Donovan realized that the greatest weakness, militarily, of our country was the lack of a permanent, wide-ranging and independent espionage organization. To be sure we had G2, the intelligence branch of the Army, and ONI which handled Naval intelligence. But they were service organizations and as such they were service-oriented, naturally interested only in the type of intelligence of immediate concern to their own type of activity. What the country needed, and desperately, argued Donovan, was a permanent intelligence setup which would provide our Government with every pertinent scrap of information necessary to the waging of all-out war, whether that information be military or naval, but certainly economic, political, social, technical, geographical, in short, complete.

In October, 1941, a scant few weeks before Pearl Harbor, the Office of the Coordinator of Information was created. Donovan was its head; he was answerable only and directly to President Roosevelt and his funds came from the President's emergency fund for security reasons. Space was allocated at 25th and E Streets on the grounds of the old National Institute of Health, a quiet little backwater not far from an old brewery in Washington.

Donovan had insisted that he meet and appraise every new member of the organization. It may have been an ideal way of building a tight group but with the explosions of recruitment that came following Pearl Harbor it became an impossibility. Everyone needed help and fast. And yet every employee had to be security checked before the work of the organization could be revealed to him.

My own career with the organization came about almost by chance. I had been serving as executive secretary to the Congressman from the capital district of Connecticut with the understanding when I went on the job at the opening of the new congressional year in January 1939 that I would stay only for the two-year term. Win, lose or draw, I did not wish to go on with a political position in Washington, or anywhere for that matter. This fact was known to Col. Edward J. Hickey, Commissioner of State Police for Connecticut and former County Detective under my father who was then State's Attorney.

Ed Hickey had known Donovan for years and one day when he was in Washington, in November 1941, lunched with him.

Donovan was full of talk about the new organization which he was just forming and told Hickey he was on the lookout for young Americans who had lived abroad and had language ability. Hickey mentioned me, said I had been schooled at Cambridge University in England and at the École des Sciences Politiques in France and had only just left Washington. The strong factor in my favor I'm sure was the fact that Donovan knew my father, having been associated with him in a couple of legal problems over the years.

At any rate, the result of the lunch between Donovan and Hickey was that Hickey made an appointment for me to meet with a Donovan assistant two days hence telling Donovan that such a meeting would of course be tentative since I knew nothing about it and might have other plans. It was agreed that if interested I would keep the appointment; if not, no harm was done.

I kept the appointment. I was hired to begin as soon as possible, which, for me, was after the first of the year. Pearl Harbor changed all that.

In my first appointments with Donovan assistants, I knew only that I was being interviewed by a new Government agency, secret in nature. What it really did, how it functioned, what I would be expected to do was a mystery. For a while, that is. Over a period of two days I was passed from one man to another until I had been seen and interviewed by a total of eighteen different people. The questions were always guarded and I'm sure that each interviewer was being cautious, circumspect and security-minded in his conversations. And perhaps if one were interviewed by only one or two persons the security would have held. As it was, any reasonably intelligent person—and the organization was attracting the intelligent—could, after a few sessions, gain a reasonably clear picture of what it was all about. By the time I had talked with all eighteen men, and some of them twice, I could almost have drawn

27

a blueprint of the organization. Which is exactly what I did for Colonel Donovan and thereby created my own job in the organization.

He was the end of the line of interviews, when at last someone had decided that I could be useful to the organization. He was standing by his desk when I was shown in, a heavyset man of medium height with thinning grey hair, sharp blue-grey eyes and a florid complexion.

"How are you, Alcorn?" He held out his hand. It was a thick, heavy hand and surprisingly soft. "And how's your father?" His voice was modulated and he looked directly at me as he spoke.

"Fine, thank you sir."

"Worked on a case with him several years ago when I was Assistant Attorney General. Always admired your father. He's done a good job in Connecticut."

I thanked him and he went on as if he hadn't heard.

"You've seen about everybody here I guess. All the branch heads, Early tells me." He turned toward a buzzer on his desk. "I'll get someone to sit down with you and go over what we do in general outline and what you can do in particular."

"But I already know, sir, pretty generally."

Colonel Donovan turned on me as if he had been electrically shocked, that quick, piercing glare of blue-grey eyes I was to learn so well.

"What do you mean? How do you know what COI does?"

"Well, I suppose I don't really, but after two days of interviews and putting the pieces together . . ."

He cut me off.

"Wait a minute." He picked up his phone. "Jimmy, come in here, right away." Almost as he replaced the receiver a slight, reddish-haired individual came in. We had met before so his glance at me was perfunctory. Donovan was talking to him as he crossed the room.

28

"Alcorn here says he has gained a pretty good idea of what COI does just from his interviews. I want you to hear what he has to say. Go ahead Alcorn, tell us what you know."

I explained how each interview fitted into place like pieces of broken crockery; how my residence and study in England occasioned only mild interest; how my residence and study in France caused deeper probing; and how my knowledge of North Africa caused so much enthusiasm that one questioner even asked if I thought I could pass as a native there. Donovan and Murphy (Jimmy) were as amused as I had been at the thought of a fair-skinned, freckled blond being agent material for North Africa. But taken together it all indicated an organization intent on operating in enemy territory in a secret manner.

Then, when I went on and described the interview in which I had been asked if I thought I could blow up a bridge, or derail a train or destroy a supply dump, Donovan and Murphy exchanged sharp looks of disbelief. They rocked with laughter when I explained how I had been asked if I thought I could arrange an assassination and had replied that I had had no prior experience.

"When can you start?" Colonel Donovan asked when I had finished. "I've got your job all cut out for you."

"Today. Now. Tomorrow. Any time you say, sir."

"Good. Report to me at eleven tomorrow. And Jimmy this is what I want. I want all potential agent personnel channelled through Alcorn until further notice. No more passing prospects around the organization, from man to man. Alcorn can get all the basic information, clear the spot security checks and then, if OK, send them on." He held out his hand to me. "We need fellows like you. I'll see you tomorrow"

It was a fascinating spot and a fast-moving one. Although the least possible publicity was given the organization, the usual Washington grapevine spread the word that a new agency was hiring and the applicants came in herds. Our screening process was simple. All applicants were requested to fill out a form giving background and experience and to leave it with the receptionist. At this point no applicant got beyond the reception room. The applications that looked promising for the intelligence setups were sent on to me and of those, the really good ones were sifted out and a spot check was made on the person by the FBI. As soon as the check cleared the person was contacted and called in for an interview. It was my job to try him out, test the real soundness of his qualifications and, if he looked like a good prospect, send him on to the proper branch head. In this way we eliminated hundreds of drifters, tightened the security of the organization and speeded up the recruiting program.

There was no independent security office in the organization in those early days with the result that all investigations of personnel were done by the FBI. In cases where speed was essential the FBI made what was called a spot-check, a quick review of all existing records for any clue as to the loyalty and reliability of the individual concerned. This was followed later with a full scale investigation the result of which was sent to Colonel Donovan in the form of a secret report. Within two weeks of my arrival at COI, Colonel Donovan had asked me to take over the reports, scan them thoroughly for him and let him know the gist of each one. For internal security reasons all of my reports to him were to be verbal, to him alone, with the result that all final decisions of hiring and firing were his. Provided the report showed nothing of a derogatory nature it was up to me to initial it for him and OK the person for further consideration.

No matter how tightly held the organization and its purpose might be, it soon became the target of every type of enemy organization for the purposes of infiltration. Communist-front organizations, Russian sympathizers, Nazi agents, Fascist agents, Jap agents, they all made crafty, sly, disarming and enticing attempts to plant personnel in our midst. One thing was known

30

of the COI, it was hiring persons with language ability and a knowledge of foreign countries and the exponents of all the various hostile "isms" tempted us with some sparkling personnel opportunities.

Like the individual who had spent the greater part of his life in the Orient in the employ of one of the larger oil companies. He had a fluent command of Chinese and Japanese, knew the countries and the people intimately and was now offering his services to the U.S. Government because he felt he could be of value to us. He sounded too good to be true. He was asked to leave an application with us and to return later for another interview. When I finally phoned him to come in again his complete file was in my desk. It showed that he had for several years been in the employ of both the Chinese and Japanese Governments as an informer and that he was at the moment suspected and wanted by the FBI as a possible Japanese agent. Three times, at the request of the FBI, I called him to the office and interviewed him while his contacts were checked out, keeping him available until the FBI could move in on him with a tight case. I felt like a Judas the last time I shook hands with him and told him we'd be in touch with him if a need for his services arose, knowing that he was walking out of my office into the custody of federal agents. I don't know what happened to him.

There was an even more glamorous episode in the very best tradition of the Mata Hari legends, so much in the pattern of the usual spy cliché that now, in retrospect, I marvel that any sophisticated agent could be so corny. It all began in the person of a small, dapper, middle-aged Frenchman who had been a naturalized American citizen for some ten years. His suits, however, were still in the French manner of wide lapels, lifted shoulders and "busy" materials and his whole appearance was too "groomed" for the American taste, greased hair and a slight aura of scent. He presented an impressive background aside from his fluent French and knowledge of the country.

31

There had been connections with large corporations and, at one time, an association with the Deuxième Bureau, the fabulous French secret service. He only wanted to help free France from German tyranny and he thought perhaps—. That was the first interview and he left the usual application.

His spot check was bad and he was called back for a second interview. A more intensive investigation turned up even more interesting material and the word was passed to keep him in view, keep him coming. A third interview was held. As he was leaving my office he mentioned, most casually, that his wife was waiting for him in the reception room and that he would like to introduce me to her. It was too good to be believed. His wife was a very pretty, very French young woman with a trim but elegant figure molded and highlighted in black satin. She stroked her dress suggestively into position over her breasts and flagged her long lashes at me invitingly. That was all.

But three days later came a long-distance call from New York. A soft, delighted voice, modulated but punctuated with those tiny high squeaks which Frenchwomen vocalize so effectively, seeped over the wires.

"Monsieur Alcorn? Ici Trixie. Trixie Boisseau."

Trixie, in her cozy manner, wondered if perhaps there was a chance Monsieur Alcorn could use her husband's services. And by the way, did Monsieur ever come into New York. It would be so nice if he could, perhaps we could dine?

Trixie could have saved her breath and the price of the phone call. Her file, and her husband's file were taking a great deal of space in my desk and they made interesting reading. They were diamond smugglers by profession, spies by avocation and at the moment they were in the employ of the German Government.

Soon afterward they both dined at the expense of the U.S. Government and enjoyed a considerable period of free lodging besides.

32

Such cases were relatively easy to handle from the standpoint of the Office of Coordinator of Information. After all the persons involved were not in the organization and whatever legal action had to be taken was taken by other agencies. But when, on occasion, a "bad apple" was discovered within the organization the problems involved became delicate and difficult to handle. The Donovan concept of the Office of the Coordinator of Information was of an office staffed by all of the most outstanding specialists of every field—economics, science, history, geography, politics, sociology, languages, press, radio and the like. Total war meant a total knowledge of the enemy and total knowledge was best served up by the top men in every field of interest.

In the early days Donovan surrounded himself only with persons whom he had known intimately and in whom he had full confidence. But as the need for more people grew it was necessary to take in his friends' friends and then their friends and so on. This brought on problems.

There was the internationally prominent figure who came into the organization with the highest backing. His spot check indicated that there might be trouble ahead but because the sponsorship was impeccable, Donovan gave the green light to put him to work. And in a fairly sensitive spot at that. When the full scale FBI investigation report finally came across my desk it contained a mass of evidence showing the subject to be actively interested in the advance of communism. I briefed Colonel Donovan on the situation and then spent the next two days, around the clock, working out a solution to the problem. At Donovan's insistence the person involved had to be removed from COI immediately but without realizing he was getting the boot. We resorted to that old haven of the Washington runaround. We made our man chairman of a planning board with a free hand to make plans and suggestions to Colonel Donovan. They were always acknowledged but never acted upon and he finally became so bored with his position he re-

33

signed. He had been with us less than three months; he was out and none the wiser. No one would have dared to guess that it would be a successful dodge, or would have worked so quickly. But then, it takes a supreme conceit to believe that one is always "kicked upstairs" because of his brilliance and not as a shelving process.

An infinitely more delicate situation involved the sister of one of the very highest officials of the then administration in Washington. She had been sent to Donovan by her brother and armed with a personal note from President Roosevelt. Only an idiot would have refused to consider an applicant so backed. Besides she was known to have a brilliant research type of mind, language ability and foreign experience. We took her on.

The spot check was disturbing. It showed a rather irresponsible identification with fringe groups but nothing really damaging. Colonel Donovan felt that it was perhaps no more than the often recognized student enthusiasm for the needling of the status quo. However, her superiors were alerted to "sterilize" her work for a time until the full report came in. And when that was finally completed it showed no more derogatory information than the original spot check.

The tempo of operations was building up, however, within the agency and Donovan became increasingly sensitive to the need for the tightest possible security. It was decided to keep a constant vigil on the lady in question, note her contacts outside of the organization and, insofar as possible, restrict the area of her work. It was a wise decision. Some few months after she had begun work with us, a night security guard surprised her as she was taking reports from an office safe and placing them in her briefcase. Any argument which she tried to make that they were only reports on which she was working and wished to take home for further study hardly held. The section in which she worked, as in most areas of the agency, forbade the removal of any papers from the building at any time for any purpose. It was Colonel Donovan personally who

34

told the young lady that her services were no longer of value to the COI.

That was unusual. Many and varied ways were used to release people from the organization but Donovan seldom, one might even say never, with the exception of the above case, became personally involved. It was remarkable that only one person openly caused trouble, and she was in a class by herself.

We had taken her on *because* of her doubtful record. She was a known Communist sympathizer at the time we hired her, but she was useful at the moment for a specialized project. However, Colonel Donovan had taken the precaution to request the FBI to keep a close watch on her activities. By that time we had our own security office within the agency and were in a position to keep the woman "sterile" in her job. At least that was the idea. But when she was told that her project was being closed out and that her services were no longer needed (no mention was made at any time of a security angle) she raised a public protest. She went to the Civil Service Commission and demanded a hearing. She gave one or two highly emotional and lurid interviews to the press knowing that publicity was the one thing we tried to avoid. She demanded a personal interview with Colonel Donovan. It was refused and he sent her to me.

Never before had I heard such profanity from a woman. She was thin and tall with grey hair and a red face, made redder by her anger. She pushed my secretary out of the way and began Goddamning the U.S. Government in general as she exploded into my office. Having covered the larger theme pretty thoroughly she took out after the COI in particular which she dubbed "a stinking Fascist organization." I broke in long enough to suggest that I couldn't understand her eagerness to stay with us feeling as she did about the outfit. This sent her into a soapboxing about rights, job preference and tenure. She talked herself into semi-exhaustion, raving, cursing and accusing in an ugly jumble of rage. When she had fin-

35

ished I rose, offered my hand, which she ignored, and showed her to the door. I haven't seen or heard of her since.

In mid-1942, there was a general upheaval in the best Washington tradition. And when the desks had finally been reshuffled and the organizational charts had been passed around, the Office of the Coordinator of Information ceased to exist. We came up with the new title of Office of Strategic Services.

Colonel Donovan was now sitting atop a lusty, burgeoning, dynamic organization stamped with his own imprint. His own energy became the energy of the OSS and just as he was most challenged by the threat of the impossible, so the organization refused to accept any project as impossible. These were the days when a conference with Donovan could take place in his car on the way to the White House or the airport. These were the days when the lights burned all night in the offices at 25th and E, Donovan's office as well as subordinates'; the days when a phone call could reach you at home at three in the morning to say, "Just a moment, the Colonel wants you." So you showered and dressed after the call and went back to work.

It looked like chaos. And I'm not sure that Donovan didn't promote the appearance of chaos as a screen to the increasing potency and effectiveness of his organization. What he had envisioned was at last beginning to work. OSS specialists were furnishing reports of every imaginable kind for the armed forces. Critical enemy areas were pinpointed, strategic areas highlighted, economic and political opportunities exploited. And to assure the current reliability of the reports, espionage agents and sabotage teams were infiltrated behind enemy lines to up-date everyone.

Donovan maintained a dynamic calm through it all. His voice was always soft, modulated at times almost to a whisper. But the quick piercing flash of the blue-grey eyes gave urgency to his words and his easy assumption that you could do the impossible made you go out and try to do it.

36

The stories of his calm approach to danger are legion but there are a few that are remarkable. There was the time we were flying into England only to find every major field in the British Isles socked in with one of the worst fogs possible. The pilot had tried everything before he alerted Donovan to our predicament. General Donovan, as he then was, was placidly going over innumerable secret reports which we had brought along for study. He looked up as the pilot stopped by his seat.

"What is it, Captain?"

"Fog, sir. We're fogged out of Prestwyck and I can't get into any other field. They're all weathered in."

"How are you on fuel?"

"An hour. Maybe a little more if we're lucky."

"Coast for awhile, and keep scanning for a field." The General turned back to his papers and went on with his reading. I was peering nervously into the murk outside, completely uninterested in the work at hand.

The General initialled a report and handed it to me.

"There must be a field down there somewhere," he said as though musing to himself.

"There's a field, all right, General. Several in fact. We just can't get on them," I replied with false facetiousness.

The pilot came back.

"Birkwood has a fifty-foot ceiling, sir. It's the only hole I can find. It's a small field and it'll be rough landing. Shall I try it?"

"Of course, Captain. But how far will we be from London if we go down there?"

"Perhaps seventy-five miles."

"Then do it. We won't mind the bumps." It never seemed to occur to him that there was any hazard involved, anything other than a routine landing.

The landing was frightful. There was no visibility at all, apparently, and they "talked" us down to a runway the pilot knew would be too short for our plane. It didn't help matters that the rest of us knew it as well. But we made it with only a few bumps and swerves and flattened bushes.

The General had worked over his paper until the very last moment before fastening his seat belt and he did that as calmly as he would lace his shoes. The plane hadn't stopped its forward motion before he had told me to get right after transportation into London. Any kind, he said, but get it.

We drove up to Claridges hours later in an Army truck and I would have given a cash reward for a record of the expression on the face of the tailcoated, cockaded doorman as General Donovan jumped over the tail gate to the ground.

It was General Donovan who made the decision to equip all agents operating behind enemy lines with our so-called "knockout" pills, lethal poison pills to be used in case of capture. In first considering the idea there seems to be something brutally inhuman in such a plan, the thought of suicide pills as standard equipment. The General's argument was anything but inhuman.

"We are dealing with life or death situations. We are using adults whom I assume to be adult enough to recognize the real meaning of self-sacrifice. In an espionage operation self-sacrifice presupposes a readiness and courage literally to sacrifice oneself by one's own hand for the protection of co-workers in a network or to insure the success of a mission. It's that simple." And then he added, "It is for the agent himself to determine, calmly and courageously, when the act of self-destruction is necessary."

He meant what he said as illustrated by the classic tale of the General waiting to get on the beaches on D-Day. He was accompanied by Col. David Bruce who was head of the OSS mission in the European Theater. Colonel Bruce, who has since been U.S. Ambassador to France and to West Germany and is currently U.S. Ambassador to Great Britain, is a tall, handsome, urbane individual with grey hair, grey eyes and an easy smile. A person of almost mannered and meticulous

38

thoughtfulness, he was an excellent counter to the Donovan impulsiveness.

In all of the mayhem, noise, confusion and turmoil that was D-Day, landing craft were lined up and shunted into the beaches much as taxis are lined up to disgorge their passengers before a theater. General Donovan was standing on his landing craft with Colonel Bruce impatiently awaiting clearance to move in. There was plenty of shooting, there were bodies bumping grotesquely against the swarming craft, there was the stench and smoke and scream and roar of battle.

"You know, David, it wouldn't be a good thing if either of us happened to be captured." He looked suddenly at Colonel Bruce.

"No it wouldn't, General."

"After all, you, as head of OSS in the ETO would be a rather good prize. And I, as over-all head of the organization would make a desirable prisoner."

Colonel Bruce nodded his agreement to what seemed basically obvious.

There was a long pause. General Donovan was probing deep into the inner pockets of his tunic, prodding himself as if to locate a certain packet, trying again and then digging deeper in another area. At last he withdrew an ordinary wallet.

"Now I have something here." His short, fully-fleshed fingers were riffling through the slots and pockets of the wallet. They sorted past papers, dove suddenly deeper and came up with a white pill. The General held it up between thumb and index finger, squinted at it, scowled and put it back in the wallet.

"No, that's an aspirin."

His fingers went on with their search and then stopped abruptly, without success.

"I must have given it to somebody," the General puzzled half to himself as he slipped the wallet back into his pocket.

Then, almost brightly, as if he had had a wonderful second thought as a solution to his problem, he turned to Colonel Bruce.

"Well, don't you worry, David. I'll shoot you first!"

He was an exhilarating person to work with. And once you had his confidence and backing you knew you had it all the way. Many times my security reports brought on unpleasant sessions with branch heads within the organization who felt that some person they happened to sponsor was being unfairly judged. But in every instance, no matter how stormy the session had been or how important the personality involved thought himself to be, Donovan backed my stand.

We had developed an excellent working arrangement by the time I was sent overseas and I had not been in the London office of OSS many weeks before the cable came through saying that 109 (Donovan's code number) was arriving and wished Alcorn assigned to him for the duration of his stay. . . . I had mixed feelings on that. I was flattered, of course, and eager to work with the General whom I sincerely liked and found stimulating. But I had a full-time job as Executive Officer to Colonel Bruce, head of OSS in the ETO and, as Special Funds Officer, the one man responsible for the financing of all secret operations on the continent, I had another full-time job.

The General arrived, was settled into a suite at Claridges, just around the corner from OSS headquarters, and I moved in with him. We were in distinguished company. Prime Minister Churchill had the penthouse. King George of Greece was there, living in exile. And King Peter of Yugoslavia with his Queen, Alexandra, and her mother, Princess Aspasia of Greece, formed another small royal court within the hotel. Loaded as it was with VIPs and the necessary security guards which their presence required in wartime London, it was amazing that the place was able to retain its air of serene elegance and not look like the armed camp it must have been.

We worked around the clock and only the fascinating and urgent character of the work made the hours endurable. We averaged about three hours of sleep a night. The General was a seven o'clock riser and, if breakfast wasn't a conference affair with one or two officers, we used it to organize our day and re-cap the previous day's work. Morning, lunch, afternoon, dinner and evenings were conferences and strategy meetings with key men in our own organization and opposite numbers from the allied espionage services. The British, the Free French, the Dutch, the Norwegians, the Danes, the Poles, the Belgians, the Yugoslavs and the Greeks, the problems were endless, delicate and complicated. Then, when the last conferee had left, usually around midnight, the General would turn to me with a delighted twinkle in his eye and say, "Now, Bob, we can get down to work." As if the day had been wasted. And for the next three or four hours we sorted out the mass of material and how it should be related to our own program.

Ten days of this kind of life brings on an intimate relationship. Shaving, showering, on the john, the work went on! I could hardly wait for his departure and I well remember it.

The General, Colonel Bruce and I had dinner together just prior to our seeing the General off by train to Scotland because fog had prevented his flying from London to Prestwyck. In the dirty, smoky, damp stink of Kings Cross station, the three of us stood outside the sleeping car in which the General had his compartment. In the blackout the tiny lights which glowed the numbers on the sleepers seemed garish and bright. It was cold and we walked back and forth and talked inconsequential talk until the whistles piped.

The General shook hands with Colonel Bruce, congratulated him again on his job and thanked him for all he had done. He took my hand.

41

"I must congratulate you, Bob. You are the first person I ever worked with without having to jump down his throat. Usually, within three days of close work, I climb all over anyone working with me." His blue-grey eyes pierced the gloom sharply and met mine. "We seem to get on all right together."

"I could tell you why, General." I returned his look and shook his hand. "You are enough like my father, temperamentally and mentally, to be his twin."

"I like that," he countered. "That's a lucky break for both of us." He boarded the train.

And I'm sure that was the key to our entire working relationship. I knew, almost before he had formed a sentence, how he was going to react to a given situation. I sensed his moods, his reflexes, his likes and dislikes, his assessment of the people we dealt with, when he would be tough, when he would be soft. He was quick to sense insincerity or pretense and he had a deep dislike for the "yes-man" type. As he said on more than one occasion, "I'd rather have a young Lieutenant with guts enough to disobey an order than a Colonel too regimented to think and act for himself."

His concept of the OSS as an efficient espionage and sabotage organization emphasized the need for unorthodox methods in planning, mounting and implementing missions. No scheme, no plan could be so fantastic that he would not give it a full hearing. And once convinced that it was a workable and productive plan, he ordered it operational as soon as possible. Harass, undermine, confuse, demoralize, penetrate, outguess the enemy, it made no difference how, so long as we were able to do it effectively.

As the organization grew and we developed agent training bases around the globe, General Donovan kept personal touch with each and every area. Although obviously, as head of the organization, a great part of his time was consumed in conferences, he was at his most effective in on-the-spot, man-to-man dealings with our agents. It could be North Africa, Burma, Italy, Ceylon, France or England, in the field the General was a tremendous morale booster. Surely, we had high-pressure brains sitting in offices in Washington evaluating reports and making them available to the proper war agencies but Donovan well knew that those reports were of little value without the effective activity of the agent. He never allowed others to forget it and certainly the success of our many missions must have come from the fact that each agent knew that the whole organization was pinpointed in on him, backing him with all its resources and alert to the dangers and responsibilities he faced.

His was the character that could coldly and with softly terse words demand the ultimate sacrifice from his men and at the same time take the trouble to carry a package or a personal message back to the agent's wife or family . . . not with any selfconscious bravado but with a natural, human concern for personal relationships. His approach was consistent. He spoke with President Roosevelt, Prime Minister Churchill, Lord Mountbatten or Alexander with the same quiet, easy confidence he used toward the GI agent and certainly in his own mind they were of equal importance in his scheme of things. It was his good fortune that this feeling was sensed by the men who worked under him and who in return gave him unquestioned loyalty.

Perhaps to one outside the organization it would seem incomprehensible that one individual could control an operation so vast and complicated as OSS. From its beginning in mid-1941 until its demise in 1946, General Donovan had developed an organization of over thirty thousand people, actively engaged in all of the war theaters and progressively effective. To say that he grew with the organization would be trite. It is more exact to point out that, in apparent chaos, he remained the calm, controlled, dynamic force able to grasp the meaning of each move, each nuance, fitted like a mosaic into one large pattern. It was his energy, his vision and his refusal to consider anything impossible which gave impetus and cohesion to

43

the outfit. Because he made himself accessible to everyone under him there developed a contact that was real, permitting him a wider grasp of his operations and personnel than most leaders enjoy. In short, to those of us to whom he became "The Wizard of OSS" he was that rare ultimate, the right man in the right place at the right time.

CHAPTER 3

"DIVINE MANIPULATION OF THE THREADS" OR MONEY MAKES THE WHEELS GO ROUND

THERE are very few "how to" books on espionage and sabotage. The reasons should be obvious. For one reason, what has once been successful under a given set of circumstances may fail under another. Both espionage and sabotage are acts of improvisation and can only generally be outlined for the beginner leaving him to devise his own methods of deception. And of course the successful agent wisely declines to reveal those elements of operation which made him successful.

It is perhaps remarkable, therefore, that one of the most concise and lucid treatises on espionage comes from the pen of Sun Tzu, a Chinese philosopher thought to have lived in the sixth century:

45

Raising a host of a hundred thousand men and marching them a great distance entails heavy loss on the people and a drain on the resources of the state. The daily expenditure will amount to a thousand ounces of silver. There will be commotion at home and abroad, and men will drop down exhausted on the highways. As many as seven hundred thousand families will be impeded in their labor.

Hostile armies may face each other for years, striving for victory which is decided in a single day. This being so, to remain in ignorance of the enemy's condition simply because one begrudges the outlay of a hundred ounces of silver in honours and emoluments, is the height of inhumanity.

One who acts thus is no leader of men, no present help to his sovereign, no master of victory.

Thus what enables the wise sovereign and the good general to strike and conquer, and achieve things beyond the reach of ordinary men, is FOREKNOWLEDGE.

Now this foreknowledge cannot be elicited from spirits; it cannot be obtained inductively from experience nor by any deductive calculation.

Knowledge of the enemy's dispositions can only be obtained from other men.

Hence the use of spies, of whom there are five classes: (1) local spies; (2) inward spies; (3) converted spies; (4) doomed spies; (5) surviving spies.

When these five kinds of spy are all at work none can discover the secret system. This is called "divine manipulation of the threads." It is the sovereign's most precious faculty.

Having LOCAL SPIES means employing the services of the inhabitants of a district.

Having INWARD SPIES, making use of officials of the enemy.

Having CONVERTED SPIES, getting hold of the enemy's spies and using them for our own purposes.

Having DOOMED SPIES, doing certain things openly for purposes of deception, and allowing our own spies to know of them and report them to the enemy.

SURVIVING SPIES, finally, are those who bring back news from the enemy's camp.

Hence it is that with none in the whole army are more intimate relations to be maintained than with spies. None should be more liberally rewarded. In no other business should greater secrecy be preserved. Spies cannot be usefully employed without certain intuitive sagacity.

They cannot be properly managed without benevolence and straightforwardness.

Without subtle ingenuity of mind one cannot make certain of the truth of their reports. Be subtle! And use your spies for every kind of business.

If a secret piece of news is divulged by a spy before the time is ripe he must be put to death together with the man to whom the secret was told.

Whether the object be to crush an army, storm a city or to assassinate an individual, it is always necessary to begin by finding out the name of the attendants, the aides-de-camp, the door-keepers and sentries of the general in command.

The enemy's spies who have come to spy on us must be sought out, tempted with bribes, led away, and comfortably housed. Thus they will become converted spies and available for our service.

It is through the information brought by the converted spy that we are able to acquire and employ local and inward spies.

It is owing to his information again that we can cause the doomed spy to carry false tidings to the enemy.

Lastly, it is by his information that the surviving spy can be used on appointed occasions.

The end and aim of spying in all its five varieties is knowledge of the enemy; and this knowledge can only be derived, in the first instance, from the converted spy. Hence it is essential that the converted spy be treated with the utmost liberality.

Hence it is only the enlightened ruler and the wise general who will use the highest intelligence of the army for the purpose of spying, and thereby achieve great results. Spies are a most important element in war because on them depends an army's ability to move.

"Liberality." That is the key and that means money. Money is the very life blood of any efficient and productive espionage

47

organization. Just as arms and ammunition are the soldier's mainstay and the symbol of his trade, so money is the ammunition with which the agent works. Certainly, since the era of Sun Tzu, the technical aspects of war have changed appallingly. One alone has facilitated espionage operations beyond his imagination—radio communication, allowing an agent to maintain contact with his base by secret code. But one thing has not changed in modern warfare and that is the basic relationship between espionage and money. Without the means to maintain a "cover" appropriate to his assignment, without funds to bribe and purchase, an agent is helpless.

It just happened to be my job to see that we had no helpless agents in the field, either for espionage or sabotage operations. It was at once a demanding, fascinating, delicate and dangerous assignment.

To the average person it would seem a simple and routine matter to finance espionage and sabotage operations behind enemy lines. The reasoning could conceivably be that all one had to do was to produce the proper amount of money in the proper type of currency and send the agent on his way. Far from it.

In modern, total war, opposing powers use not only military weapons but economic, social and political measures to unbalance each other. All normal currency exchange between belligerents ceases. Where money is concerned the relationship between belligerents is at its most fantastic.

This can best be substantiated by pointing out that the bulk of French francs used by the OSS for its agent operations against the Axis originally came out of France by German planes from Stuttgart. Fantastic? Of course. And unbelievable but true.

The disappearance of normal currency exchanges brought on the black market in belligerent currencies. In order to illustrate what happened when the OSS went into the black market, let us follow the trail of a thousand franc note, serial No.

P-2475-843. This note was printed by the Bank of France in 1936. Because the German Government was as anxious to obtain foreign currencies for subversive operations against the allied Governments as we were to obtain currencies for operations against Germany, the Germans facilitated the flow of French currencies into neutral countries. Germany was in the market in Lisbon for escudos which could later be converted into dollars or sterling. And because OSS had created a market for francs in Lisbon it was to the interest of the German Government to see that francs reached Lisbon for exchange against other currencies more advantageous to its operations.

Let us say that note P-2475-843, a Bank of France issue originated in Paris. It is, along with thousands of others, packaged and sent on to Stuttgart for consignment to Lisbon. In Stuttgart it is put aboard a Lufthansa plane for Lisbon where it arrives in payment against escudo credits. An OSS agent, on instruction from OSS London, through a carefully developed chain of "cut-outs," comes into possession of note P-2475-843 along with others which he has purchased for our use. The note arrives in London where it is checked against our listings of suspect currencies and marked issues.

P-2475-843 is found to be safe and is packed with others for issue to an agent being dropped into France for espionage operations against Germany. In the performance of his mission, it is quite possible that our OSS agent may put note P-2475-843 into circulation as part of a bribe for the express purpose of eliminating an agent of the Gestapo. The note has gone full circle and the German Government has directly assisted in the elimination of one of its own agents.

To forestall the possibility of a similar situation being turned against allied agents, OSS operated in the black market almost entirely in foreign currencies or gold, rather than dollars or sterling. Every possible effort was made to keep dollars out of the hands of the enemy and for that reason we utilized other means. Gold, of course, was the ideal for operating in the black market for once it got into the hands of a black market operator it was withdrawn from circulation and could be assumed as buried for the duration.

It is only natural, in thinking of espionage operations, that one considers secret agents infiltrating enemy territory for the purpose of obtaining military and strategic information. Certainly that is the basic raison d'etre. It is rarely realized that to supply those agents with the money vital to their missions it is first necessary to run agent operations of an even more complicated and delicate nature. In short, before our producing espionage or sabotage agents could function, other currency agents had to obtain the wherewithal. Those who operated from the neutral countries like Spain, Portugal, Switzerland or Sweden, where one could rub elbows with the enemy, could operate with a certain amount of freedom. Undercover, of course, and with the greatest possible attention to secrecy and security. But there were agents who had to operate within the enemy countries in order to keep us informed of any currency manipulations calculated to entrap our espionage or sabotage agents.

Carl was perhaps our most effective currency agent. And we got him through impeccable sources. Even prior to 1939 and the outbreak of hostilities, Carl, who was German born and bred, was an avowed anti-Nazi with enough intelligence and skill to hide his aversion to the Hitler regime with success. It was our great bit of luck that he was an officer of one of the larger banks in Berlin. The situation was made to order because he was in that second echelon of officers, real working personnel, so necessary to the financial operations of the bank that he was service exempt; he had been with the bank for many years; and he was completely informed as to its operations. Even before we came into the war, Carl had seen what was coming and contact was made which could be imple-

50

mented when hostilities started. In effect, contact was really never broken although there were periods in the early part of the war when long silences gave us some concern.

To my knowledge Carl utilized only two agents, both of them French and both of them personnel of the Bank of France. It was the perfect arrangement for our purposes. It was a lucky thing we had them.

The Germans played the most diabolical games with foreign currencies, most especially the French franc. From Carl we learned that the Nazis guessed that most agent activity on our part would be through France and they therefore concentrated on attempts to snare our agents through invalid or recalled bills. Obviously, the five-thousand-franc note would be the principal target for two reasons. The issuance of five-thousand-franc notes was not so great that it couldn't be fairly rigidly controlled; and obviously the five-thousand-franc note was of most value to agent operations because it permitted the issuance of large sums without too much bulk.

At first the Nazis were naïve enough to try marking bills. This they did in different ways; the use of a slightly heavier pressure on a number; the shadings of a figure on the bill; a clipped end or a peculiar perforation. This was good in theory but they found that it was impossible to forewarn enough outlets with any amount of secrecy with the result that the marked bills were freely passed and could be fifth or sixth hand by the time they were recognized. Any tracing back to the agent was almost impossible.

They then, suddenly, would declare a series invalid and notify all banks to hold anyone offering a bill from an invalidated series. This was partially effective but it made our agents more wary in the use of large denominations for current operations and they simply hoarded them for bribe money if they were not assured of their safety.

At one point the Germans circulated the rumor through

51

France that all five-thousand-franc notes were to be recalled. This rumor circulated and subsided almost periodically and it caused us some concern but the action was never put into effect.

Actually, the most effective and disturbing ruse used was dreamed up by the Gestapo. Its cleverness lay in the fact that it made every bank and post office in France an unwitting assistant in an attempt to trap allied agents. The ruse ran something like this:

A particular issue of notes, the numbers of which had been retained by the Gestapo, were sent into the black market in a neutral country, practical assurance that they would eventually find their way into the hands of agents being sent into France. The Gestapo then set out warning to all banks and post offices in France that a bank robbery had been perpetrated and that notes of a specific series had been taken. All banks and post offices were notified that should any note of this series be passed the Gestapo should be informed immediately. The banks and post offices, operating in perfectly good faith and innocently supposing that they were assisting in the capture of bona fide bank robbers, made every effort to comply with this request.

In this manner the Gestapo foiled any possible collaboration between someone in a bank or post office and an agent. An agent attempting to pass such a note would be arrested immediately.

Carl helped us avoid these traps. And only once did our timing come close to disaster. We had several notes of a hot series in our possession and ready for agent use when the intelligence came in that they were marked and we withdrew them from circulation. How did we get the news? One of Carl's agents, who almost "commuted" between London and Paris during our busiest periods, and this prior to the landings in France, brought us the serial numbers in microdots. He carried no papers of any kind that would be incriminating if he was captured. He and Carl had been more clever than that. The agent had several small dark moles on different parts of his body. It was quite simple to add two or three more, depending on the volume of our correspondence at the moment, which, when developed and blown up, brought us what we needed to know!

The problem of obtaining reichsmarks was greater than any we faced, certainly more difficult than obtaining French francs. If the Nazis can be admired for anything, they can probably be most complimented on the rigid control which they exercised with respect to the circulation of their own currencies.

The difficulty was created because of the fact that four types of German currency were in circulation and yet three of these four types had certain circulating restrictions within Germany or German-occupied territory which rendered them useless to agent operations. There was the reichscreditkassen note, originally issued for circulation within Germany as small change. It later became occupation currency and was used almost exclusively in occupied Poland in the early days of the war. Subsequently a reichscreditkassenscheine note was issued as a "soldier" currency for the payment of troops and to be used by troops for purchases in foreign countries. They were revoked in France on December 15, 1943. They were never circulated in Denmark, Norway, Holland, Croatia or Greece, but were used for a short time in Serbia and withdrawn. For some time they were recognized as official currency in Ostland and in Transistria under Rumanian jurisdiction as well as in certain areas of Yugoslavia. There was a nightmare of danger involved in their use or possession.

The third note was the rentenbank note. This series was originally issued in denominations of 1, 2, 5, 10, 50, 100 and 1000 marks. These were rendered useless for agent operations because of the fact that from October 1, 1942, all rentenbank notes above the five-mark note were declared invalid. To equip an agent with any sizeable amount of these funds would be impossible simply because of the bulk involved.

This left us with only the fourth type, the reichsbank note, which could be used freely and safely for agent operations within Germany proper. These notes were issued in denominations of 10, 20, 50, 100, 500, and 1000. They were the most difficult to obtain owing to the strict controls maintained by the German Government but we did get them in sufficient quantities for the use of our agents. It was frustrating to know that Carl was sitting in Berlin, handling thousands of these notes daily and yet unable to send any to us. However, he was much too valuable in all his other capacities without running the risk involved in supplying us the money itself. He did, though, discover a rather surprising source in the Bank of France where we bought notes at an exorbitant figure, notes which the Bank of France had obtained from French forced labor groups returning to France from Germany.

Almost anyone who has ever been connected with the running of an agent operation in enemy territory would admit that the most dangerous, single potential in an agent's work is his money. It was our job to see that all monies issued to an agent were safe, usable and in no way suspicious. Without belaboring the detail involved in accomplishing this, one example of the type of problem to be faced should be sufficient.

Frequently, when a large shipment of French francs came into OSS in London, there would be many bundles of new notes, serial numbers running in sequence and obviously fresh from the Bank of France. One of the first things to be done was to check the numbers against our lists of "hot" issues. Next the sequences had to be broken and shuffled in with other issues already at hand. Then began the tedious process of "pinholing." This calls for explanation.

54

New notes issued by the Bank of France are naturally fresh and unmutilated. It must be borne in mind that Bank of France notes in this condition are available only to banks in France or to accredited Government agencies. The very fact that an individual should have in his possession a new, *unblemished* note would arouse suspicion. It is the custom in French banks to count notes on receipt from the Bank of France and to pin the notes together with a common pin into small bundles or packets. It is obvious, therefore, that any bank note which has had proper circulation in France through regular channels will show at least two pin holes and, in many cases, more. It was up to us to see that every note which we issued to an agent had at least one pair of the telltale pinholes! A ridiculously minor detail? Perhaps, but agents have been trapped on less.

Another problem we faced was the aging of notes quickly, artificially, without having them look as if they had been purposely rumpled. We tried innumerable methods, even to the rubbing of them with soil, a procedure which left a detectable dirt residue which we didn't like. Our final solution caused some amusement among our office personnel. We found that the best possible way to age new bills was to scatter them on the floor of a room in which persons were carrying on routine duties over a period of hours. After they had been walked on and generally scrubbed about under foot they took on the appearance of bills long in circulation. It was our practice, therefore, to lock an inner office, scatter one to five million francs about the floor, and go on with the day's work. A day or two of this treatment rendered them innocuous in the hands of an agent operating in the field.

It was a source of considerable pride on the part of the small group in OSS responsible for these secret currency operations that, in the entire war, no agent was lost or revealed because of any error in the funds with which he was provided.

This contrasts sharply with that incredible operation in the summer of 1942 when the Germans landed two different groups of four-man saboteur teams on the American East Coast. And a part of the funds which had been provided them were in U.S. gold certificates which had been recalled by executive order in 1933!

There is a second, greater danger in the money element. That is its use. In conversations with persons of long experience in the handling of agents' funds, one fact will always stand out. Invariably, when an agent is "blown" he is "blown" because he has been unwise in the use of his money. Let's use an example which we often put before agents in training before they left on a mission:

Jean Pierre is to be dropped into France for the purpose of organizing resistance groups. Weeks of painstaking care have gone into the preparation of his mission. Attention has been given to the most minute details in documents, clothing, accessories and all of the elements of a carefully drawn cover story. Let us suppose that Jean Pierre is to go into a small town in the middle of France with instructions to set himself up in a small shop of some description. Let us say that from prior experience he is capable of running a bakery. He buys a small bakery. He allays any suspicion with a carefully thought-out cover story as to why he should suddenly appear in this particular small town as a baker. He succeeds in the first elements of his mission; he gains the confidence of the people around him and his life settles into the routine pattern of normalcy which is so vital to the success of a good agent.

Prior to departure for his mission Jean Pierre has been supplied with one million French francs. Only those bank notes which are absolutely sound and unquestioned and which may circulate freely in the area in which he is to operate are provided him. New bills have been aged, pin-holes have been checked, serials have been verified safe. He has a variety of denominations and they are packaged for his convenience, some for his immediate use, some to be buried. The briefing officer has been careful to go over all the essential details of his mission, and has cautioned him to handle his money discreetly. He has also advised him to hide a great portion of his funds for future operations and escape.

Jean Pierre establishes himself soundly as a baker and, at the end of six or eight weeks, feeling somewhat safer in his new environment, he begins to circulate more freely and to enlarge the scope of his activity. He is constantly aware of the fact that he has a large amount of money at his command—very likely more actual cash and purchasing power than he has ever had at his disposal before. Jean Pierre imagines that it is essential to his mission that he contact agent "X" in Paris or some other large city distant from his base. Without further thought he proceeds into town. He goes because he has the money and the means of accomplishing the trip. But does the average baker in the average small town in the middle of France ever get to Paris?

Once that question is raised and once the natives begin to wonder as to how the baker, Jean Pierre, manages a few days in Paris, a weakness appears in the cover of our agent. He may be guilty of only the one indiscretion. But the good agent, the agent who produces and lives to return to his base, must never raise doubt. The very fact that Jean Pierre failed to recognize that a small-town baker in the middle of France has a limited income and therefore, necessarily limited movement, may well be responsible for his discovery and the failure of his mission.

It becomes an eroding process. The first surprised comment may come from an innocent and friendly neighbor, passed in daily gossip among friends. But in wartime, as so many vivid posters in England emphasized, doors and furniture, houses and trees, everything has ears and it only takes one pair of enemy-oriented ones to turn the quiet glow of suspicion on our agent. Once under surveillance, the chances of his ultimate success are nil. Jean Pierre has betrayed himself.

Agent financing would drive the average bank executive insane. Apart from the vast inventory of cash in various foreign currencies that had to be maintained, the exchange rates were a nightmare of inconsistency. Some currencies, obtained through regular finance channels, were carried at the established rate. Some were carried at the going black market rate, which can change with the weather. And some, confiscated by operating agents from enemy installations, were carried as manna from Heaven, a budget bonus. In short, in the life and death battle of wits necessary to assure funds for clandestine operations in wartime, anything goes.

Under the authority granted the OSS the secret funds were an outright grant and were subject to no accounting of any kind. This was an obvious security measure. In the first few months of its existence, OSS funds came from the President's emergency fund, and they were doled out by the President as they were needed with no questions asked. Then, as the OSS grew and flourished, a separate budget was established. The funds made available to the organization under the proper appropriation were labelled "unvouchered." That was the key word, for it meant that no other agency of the Government had any authority whatsoever to demand an accounting for the expenditure of the monies involved. It was assurance that no scrutiny would ever be made of how these funds were spent. It was most vital to the success of the operations of OSS for, like tracing a river to its source, the flow of secret money could divulge the whole vast network of OSS.

The very fact that the organization was given complete latitude and discretion in the use of these funds imposed a tremendous responsibility on General Donovan and the men under him who were charged with the actual handling and expenditure of untold millions. For this reason, highly secret records were kept within the organization showing the cost of missions, the money allocated to various projects, and the like. And with it all, an enormous and complicated effort was made to reconcile the incredible inconsistencies of black market rates, valuation of unmounted precious stones, items of jewelry, and related bribe and exchange media.

London offered practically the only war zone where any semblance of routine banking could be followed. Everywhere else we were on a strictly cash basis. But in London we were able to establish bank accounts and use checks for some of the items that did not involve security to a dangerous degree. However, these accounts were carried as the personal accounts of the Special Funds officer. I've often wondered what some of London's more conservative bankers thought a young American officer was doing in a war area with hundreds of thousands of dollars in extremely active checking accounts. And yet they were seeing only the thinnest edge of the coin.

Millions in cash in dozens of foreign currencies passed through the Special Funds officer's hands for the implementation of the expanding espionage and sabotage missions. As far as the Government was concerned it could have been thrown into the air. But within the OSS itself the Special Funds branch could show at a glance where the bulk of the money was being spent, what operations were expensive, what ones were ridiculously cheap, what ones had, surprisingly, paid for themselves by the sudden "liberation" of enemy cash. Currency inventories, gold inventories, jewels and the like, they were all there in a top secret file for our own enlightenment—and protection.

Then, as the organization grew and its operations became more complex and intertwined, a full scale international secret banking system developed within the OSS. From Washington the lines reached out around the world until we were able to finance our operations by code cable between such vastly separated areas as Chungking and London or Lisbon and Calcutta. The idea was to service the missions. It mattered little how or

59

from what base so long as the funds were available and in sufficient amount.

Just as blood courses through a body and gives it life, so money must flow within an espionage network and give it impetus. We had the money in abundance. We pumped it into the secret veins of the OSS body to make that body effective. It bought us information. It bought us resistance groups and partisans. It helped to bring us victory.

CHAPTER 4

THE CASBAH

THE STENCH was oppressive.

Rotting garbage, excrement, urine, the decaying flesh of some small animal left to bloat and disintegrate where it had fallen, the all-pervading smoke waves of burning incense and tobacco, almost indecent with musk, the whole made the more unendurable by the burning intensity of the sun and the parched red-brick hardness of the bare earth. The narrow, now dark-shadowed, now sun-blazed streets were filled with people. Full-bearded men in long robes, women robed and veiled, naked children, they seemed to move silently and with sinister stealth through the miasma. And everywhere were the flies, large, green-black glistening obscenities which rose in clouds from every scrap of offal and filth in the teeming labyrinth.

Selim moved with the crowd, covering his nostrils against the stink and yet knowing as he did so that in such slight action could he make himself conspicuous. And he wondered instinctively if the others didn't notice the smells or whether they ignored them or endured them and accepted them as he never could. His white jellaba billowed behind him as he walked swiftly along the street and he gathered it around him, drawing its folds partly across his face.

There was a difference about Selim but it was a difference which didn't show on the surface. That was the reason for his presence now in the Medina, the teeming, squalid Arab quarter of Casablanca. Selim was the son of a French mother and an Arab father, a mixture which, in Algiers, would have branded him as a "colon." He was dark skinned, with the black eyes and hair of the Arab but, until now, his life had been oriented away from the Arab world. He had been schooled in France and he had absorbed French culture and manners, French life, as more agreeable to him than the Arab environment in which he was growing. And yet he could mix and live in the Arab world with all the ease and freedom of the full-blooded native.

The Allied landings in North Africa, the shame of the Vichy regime, the Darlan fiasco and the Giraud Government, these coupled with the idealist drive and burning eagerness of youth had driven Selim to OSS. Not that he knew of OSS. He had never heard of the organization or knew of its existence until, after scrutiny, security checks and study, he was approached by one of our men in Casablanca. He was ripe for our picking and he volunteered enthusiastically to work with us.

So now he was in the Medina, braving the stench and the heat.

Fortunately, life in the Medina moved slowly. The natives neither walked nor strolled, they ambled, slowly, aimlessly.

Only the shifting, darting of the eyes showed any alertness of nature. It suited Selim to amble for his mission called for slow, step by step probing of the area.

Some weeks prior to this day our D-F-ing apparatus had picked up disturbing short-wave signals. The apparatus consisted of a couple of mobile radio installations hidden in ordinary beat-up old trucks which could be driven inconspicuously through the city. Listening for the clandestine transmitters, the trucks, by cross-bearings on their signals, could fairly accurately zero in on a secret installation. It didn't take much checking of codes and transmitters to discover that an enemy sending station was operating somewhere within the city of Casablanca.

However, it is in the nature of such secret operations to be mobile, irregular in transmission and, for those reasons, difficult to uncover. The Casablanca transmitter was elusive. Twice we had what we thought was a definite fix but each time we had been cheated and there was nothing to be found when the pinpoint was checked. But now the signals, still elusive, still playing cat and mouse, were coming from that vast, stinking labyrinth known as the Medina, where no cars could go because the narrow, winding, crowded nature of the alleys made such D-F-ing procedure impossible. Selim was briefed for the mission.

And he was given an accomplice.

Bada was the black to Selim's white. Where Selim had education and refinement, Bada had only basic schooling and crudeness. Where Selim had manners and compassion, Bada had craft and toughness to the point of cruelty. But they both had courage, a sense of dedication and a loyalty to each other. Bada, almost twice the age of Selim, had worked all his life for Selim's family and had, literally, carried Selim on his shoulders from his infancy. It was a natural team. Trained in OSS schools, they were the ideal pair for the job that lay ahead.

Selim could feel the warm pressure of the small apparatus

strapped under his arm and concealed by the loose folds of his jellaba. A tiny wire led from it to a small plug in his right ear and he had wrapped a part of the garment up over his shoulder and across his head to cover the tiny mechanism. Not as powerful as the mobile D-Fs used in the trucks, these small gadgets were the brain child of an OSS radio expert and they more than made up for the loss of scope by their adaptability to this type of operation.

The signals had been coming in strong and clear when first Selim had entered the Medina and it was this fact that had occasioned his first hurried progress. But then, lest his eagerness betray him, he had slowed to the native amble, watching the passing crowds, wondering what circuitous route Bada might be taking from another angle and waiting for the beep of the signals.

Past cupboard-like shops displaying brasses, leather goods, silver work, rugs. Past the vegetable and fruit stalls with their flies. Past the hanging carcasses and blood-covered trays of rotting meat shimmering green-black with flies and stinking of decay. Past old men, singly and in groups, sitting on the bare dirt and smoking languidly into the distance. Past black-eyed women, so heavily veiled they looked like walking pillars of piece goods with eyes, somehow all of them looking mysteriously beautiful because the ugliness of a crooked nose or a gap-toothed mouth was hidden. Past knots of naked, dirty children urinating in the streets, stealing fruits or playing crude games among the crowds. Past scores of wandering, mangy, half-starved dogs. Past all of these and more. And all the while, now steady, now intermittent, the beeping code of the secret transmitter.

Then, as suddenly as the first beeps had been picked up, there was silence. Selim walked on, waiting, hoping, anxious to find it and have it over with but to no avail.

Two hours later he gave up in despair. He and Bada would have to try again another day.

And they did, the very next day. With mixed emotions.

He hated the Medina. He hated the filth and the stench, the spectacle of humans living almost like animals only often with less dignity. But he tingled with the excitement of the challenge and he went in search of the clandestine sending station much as one would stalk rare game.

They were there early, before there had been any telltale beeps from the hidden operator. This time they had changed areas, Selim taking that part of the maze which Bada had covered the preceding day, Bada working over the same general area that Selim had surveyed.

Silence. As the morning grew old and the sun burned to the blistering point, Selim patrolled the Medina, his ear almost aching with anticipation of the first signal. Still there was silence. He stopped at a coffee stall, squatted on the dirt and ordered a cup of black, thick coffee. It was almost like syrup and he let it stand on its tiny brass tray before him until it was quite cool. He watched the passing crowd almost absently, raised the cup to his lips and drank.

So strong was the signal he felt he must have reacted noticeably. He held his cup half raised to his lips and waited. There it was again, clear, strong and—close. He tried to control the excitement he felt rising within himself. He could almost hear his brain repeating the training he had received: "Never give yourself away by any sudden action not easily explained to the casual observer." He took another sip of the coffee, slowly, paused a moment and then drained the cup. As if he had all the time in the world, he rose, paid for the coffee and walked up the narrow alley.

The signals were coming now regularly but they seemed to weaken slightly as he walked. He must change direction but he dared not go back past the coffee stall. He took a side alley and doubled back in the general direction of the coffee stall. The signals were strong again.

The street before him was narrow and winding and it sloped uphill. It was less crowded than the area he had just left and it was lined on both sides with small cubicles which were so alike they seemed to have been mass-produced by some enormous assembly line. Each cubicle was dark but through the gloom one could see a bed and a chair. The floor was of dirt, there was a curtain of rough material hanging from the top of the door frame and drawn back to disclose the interior and, flowing past the doors, on either side of the street, were open drains which stank and were slime-covered. Young girls leaned against some of the door posts and as he approached, Selim was conscious of their excitement and activity. They called to him, motioned to him with open palms and then spat at him as he passed unnoticing. They chattered to each other like so many monkeys, shouting obscenities to one another and making disgusting gestures. One girl, Selim thought she could have been no more than fourteen, ran eagerly toward him and then, when not six feet away, stopped, raised her skirt high above her head and exposed her naked body.

"Baksheesh," she screamed at him as he pushed past her, and then spat a mouth full of saliva and obscenity after him.

The signals were stronger. Intermittent now, but strong, and he moved slowly up the narrow street. Still the enticements, the chattering and the obscenities.

Suddenly, just ahead, there was loud coarse laughter, screams of delight, more laughter and giggles. It grew louder as he approached and then, through the door of one of the cubicles, burst three naked bodies. They were rolling over and over in the dirt, through the slime of the stinking gutters and into the middle of the street, two men and a girl. Only when they came to rest against the wall of the opposite buildings did they seem to realize where they were. Amid more laughter and obscenities, they got up, threw their arms around each other and disappeared back into the house from which they had come.

66

The signals were now loud and steady. And it seemed to Selim that they had increased almost to a crescendo during the revolting scene in the street. He went on, one, two, three cubicles, four. The signals began to fade. He hesitated, half turned and then waited.

Then, up ahead, he saw him.

Walking slowly, chatting, pausing, peering into each cubicle as he came on, was Bada. His jellaba was thrown well over his shoulder and he was holding a part of it across his face as if to ward off the heat of the sun. If he noticed Selim in the crowd he gave no sign of it.

Selim now was breathing heavily from the excitement of the chase and the realization that their quarry was so near at hand. But where?

He paused, turned and started slowly back the way he had come. There was a renewed flurry of activity among the girls in the doorways—the shopper was returning, perhaps to buy— and Selim blessed them all for covering the true purpose of his stroll.

Again the signals were louder and he paused before a door. From the corner of his eye he could see Bada coming slowly down the street toward him and instinctively he wondered why he didn't hurry. He had a wild impulse to call out to him.

A girl came toward him, waving and motioning indecently, and he started to move on. The cubicle before him was open and like all the others there was a bed and a chair. A young girl was seated on the chair as if exhausted, head down, eyes half closed. She seemed unaware of his presence until, out of the shadow of the cubicle a voice spoke to her. Selim peered in at the sound. There, seated cross legged on the floor in the corner was an enormous heap of a woman. Covered as she was with veil and jellaba, she could have been any age, any shape but she was obviously enormous.

The girl rose from her chair and came forward. Selim hesitated. The signals had ceased abruptly. This could be it. But how? Where?

A couple of unintelligible grunts came from the woman on the floor and the girl snapped back at her sharply. Then, suggestively, she started to slide her skirt slowly up the length of her bare leg.

The older woman was now staring at Selim and she was pulling the folds of her jellaba around her protectively. It was a natural gesture and yet somehow a trifle too concentrated to be casual. Selim spoke to her and smiled and then, as the woman shifted position on the floor, a quick glint of light caught his eye and he saw it. A tiny trail of wire slithered out from behind the woman. Selim moved inside a pace, spoke again, and glanced around the room.

It was there. No bigger than a thread, the wire ran up a corner of the wall and made a circuit of the room at ceiling level. One, two, perhaps three circuits of the room, whatever had been deemed necessary for an adequate aerial, the wire was carefully strung around the small cubicle.

The young girl was now clinging to his arm, enticing him, when he saw the doorway shadowed. He half turned, ready to withdraw and wait for Bada, knowing he would have to move quickly and surely and yet hesitant. The decision was made for him.

Without a sound, as he had turned away, the huge bulk of a woman lunged at him from the floor. She caught him off balance and dragged him down and in a moment they were rolling in a death struggle on the dirt. The girl bit him on the leg, tore and dug at him and then he could feel the huge weight of the older woman pressing him down, could feel the clutch of strong hands reaching for his throat while he fought and struggled to free himself.

In terror he saw the horrible, piercing eyes coming closer and closer as the strangling grip on his throat made a cracking

68

sound in his ears. Then, as the clothing had fallen away in the struggle, as the veil had been ripped away, he realized that the face now close to his and the hands at his throat belonged to a man. He felt that he was about to black out when, as suddenly as it had begun, the terrible pressure relaxed, there was a quick, quiet sobbing gasp and the huge figure fell away from him and he was free.

Standing over the two of them was the heavy breathing figure of Bada. He was almost casually wrapping the garrotte around his hand.

"That was quick." He helped Selim to his feet.

Selim brushed his clothes and looked around him. The place was a shambles. The "woman" was prostrate across the floor. It was the body of a large man, the face now the grotesque grimace of a victim of strangulation. The enormous figure, under the ample jellaba, proved to be transmitting equipment. The "bosom" was an ingenious sending apparatus and everything else necessary to an efficiently clandestine radio operation was there, part of the make-up of the "woman." The aerial, cleverly hidden and charcoal dusted to kill the gleam of metal, circled the room twice and would have gone unnoticed by the casual visitor.

Together, Selim and Bada gathered up the equipment, concealed it under their robes and tucked it under their arms. They pulled the aerial from the wall, rolled the thin wire and took that with them as well. In his turn, each one glanced carefully around the small room, over the bed, the chair, the floor, the grotesque body of the man and at the girl. She was lying where Bada had left her, in the corner, just inside the door. Selim thought she looked younger and even pretty, her lifeless face not contorted. They slipped out into the sunshine.

It was blazing bright. There were people still passing up and down the alleys and the girls were chattering, calling, luring and making their indecent suggestions. Selim and Bada ignored them.

With the surging, tingling desire to run, at least to walk swiftly, churning within them, they ambled down the narrow street.

That evening the message went out to OSS Algiers and other outposts interested—CLANDESTINE ENEMY TRANSMITTER—CASABLANCA—OFF THE AIR.

CHAPTER 5

THE PLANNERS

ONE SHOULD not get the impression that agent operations were spontaneous affairs. It would be absurd to think that we simply dropped agents into enemy territory with the instructions "go find some intelligence." That would be like cutting them adrift on an open sea. Rather, every agent mission began with a specific problem to be solved, a definite question to be answered and was developed from there.

In the early days of the war, through most of 1942, the plans were made in Washington. Then, as the war progressed and the emphasis moved into the European Theater with an OSS base in London, more projects were initiated and implemented from there. To state simply that it was a complex operation would be rash understatement.

71

Two separate branches within the organization carried the burden. One, the Research and Analysis branch, blossomed almost overnight into a high-powered operation involving the best brains the country could produce. Originally headed for a short period by Dr. James Phinney Baxter, former president of Williams College, it really began to roll, burgeon and produce under the leadership of Dr. William L. Langer, chairman of the history department at Harvard.

But to fill in the picture from my own angle so that the chronology is not lost, it would be best to emphasize the fact that by mid-1942 the organization was expanding vigorously, new shifts in duty and chain of command were evolving and new organizational lines were being drawn. Although I was still operating as originally with General Donovan, a new personality had come into the picture at the executive level.

William H. Vanderbilt, former Governor of Rhode Island, now a Navy Commander, came into the organization to head all administrative services under General Donovan. Tall, quiet, unassuming, Commander Vanderbilt took over the job of trying to make chain-of-command sense out of a mushrooming organization. It was for him to see that the various branches got the space they needed to function, the personnel necessary to function and the co-ordinated cooperation of a variety of temperament. It was a monumental task.

Obviously he needed help and he needed it on the spot in each of the branches. Therefore, under the chain-of-command set-up, Commander Vanderbilt had a representative within each branch responsible for his operation and answerable to him and to the branch chief as well. I was tapped for the job with Research and Analysis and moved into an office next to Dr. Langer, affectionately referred to in the organization as "Bull" Langer.

Dr. Langer *was* a great bull of a man. Of medium height, he was heavily set with a massive head which seemed to sit on his shoulders without benefit of a neck. He had a thick,

72

bristling head of wire-straight hair, heavy features and a booming voice which seemed to roar even in a whisper. A recognized authority on modern European history, Dr. Langer now found himself in charge of producing for OSS the ultimate in knowledge for use against the enemy.

Under him, within the Research and Analysis branch, there developed an economics division, a political science division, a geography division, a North African division, a Far Eastern division, a sociology division and a psychology division. These in turn were serviced by photographic, cartographic and microfilm sections, index, reference and chart sections and transport and industrial sections. It was like a small university staffed by the most highly specialized brains in each field but with a difference. Instead of pupils to preach to and instruct, the brains produced their studies for more brains to digest, sift, assimilate and congeal into information on which espionage, sabotage and military, naval and air operations could be mounted.

There were bound to be clashes of temperament and there were many, some of them so childish as to try the credulity of almost anyone. Like the day I had come back to my office from a conference out of the building to find my secretary in a flurry of excitement. It seems that one of our eminent specialists, a man who had headed his own department at one of the top universities and was now running a division for us, had been calling for me on the phone at regular intervals which seemed to her to have been every thirty seconds. His message was that I was to come to his office immediately on my return.

I could hear his loud, complaining voice as I approached his office, so that I was somewhat prepared for a difficult session. However, I was far from ready for the spectacle I waded into. The professor's secretary, distraught and harried, simply opened the door to his inner office, let me inside and closed the door behind me. She was careful to be on the other side of the door.

73

The "doctor", authority in his field, author of textbooks and learned treatises, division head, was seated in the middle of the office floor. He was shouting as I came in and he was beating the rug with his fists in a fit of temper much more in keeping with a spoiled child of three. His egg bald head was reddened and glistening with perspiration and he peered at me through his rimless spectacles with a wildly enraged look.

I found it embarrassing to stand looking down at him and suggested that he might be more comfortable in a chair at his desk while we discussed his problem. He turned on me in a fury, swearing that he would never again sit at his desk until he had a better one to use. So he remained on the floor, and in the manner of a petulant child, told me his story.

It seems that that very morning the learned professor had gone into the office of another one of our professor-specialists for a conference. It so happened that this second professor had worked under the distraught doctor at their former university, was junior to him in service at the university, junior in years and, certainly in the estimate of the doctor himself, junior in learning. But, and this was the dreadful thing, the junior professor was seated behind a larger desk than the one furnished the bald doctor and it was elaborately carved! Prestige!

As soon as the doctor had returned to his own office he had telephoned the supply office and asked for a carved desk. This was a matter of such importance he had not entrusted it to his secretary but had made the call himself. It was all the more infuriating, then, to have, as he said, "some uneducated, civil service underling," tell him that he could not have another desk but would have to keep the one he had. It seemed there was a war going on, there were many fast growing agencies and Washington was running low on carved desks.

The result was the tantrum. This learned Ph.D. had slammed down the telephone, decamped to the middle of his floor and shouted to his secretary to call me immediately. It hadn't helped matters to find that I was unavailable for at least a half hour. But there he was, refusing to sit at a plain, ordinary desk which he now considered unsuitable to his eminence.

Fortunately, I had been exposed to other petty jealousies within the branch although I must admit this topped them all. Feeling slightly silly, I patiently explained that it would be most difficult to get hold of another desk, certainly a carved one, and that any attempt at a change might, horrible to contemplate, produce a desk inferior even to the one he already had. Then, much as one would impose a stern ruling on a spoiled child, I announced that I had no intention of doing anything about another desk. I left the office in the midst of another surge of temper tantrum.

The professor made it back to his desk sometime during the afternoon.

It was an enlightening experience, my association with the Research and Analysis branch. The pecking order was brutal. It was almost an insult to address any one as professor. To a man all those eligible insisted on being called doctor. It got so bad that the rest of the organization, to the amusement of General Donovan, referred to the building which housed R & A as the "medical school."

Vanity seemed to rule the whole setup. In several instances, men of high standing in their particular field were given key spots as division heads. Then, when another scholar in the same field became available, it was decided that one could not be placed above the other in the chain of command. So a new board or committee would be established for the late arrival from which he could function without having to take orders from his colleague. It was essential to give such a board or committee a pompous title such as the Board of Analysts or the Board of Review but to those in the know it was only a dodge, a rather tawdry and pathetic one when you realize that it was played out against the background provided by the Battle of Midway, the Coral Sea, Okinawa and the like.

As the branch grew, each doctor brought in his research

75

assistants from his former university. Then, when they were used up, the prize pupils, the "teacher's pets," were brought in to do the work. This latter move caused the General some uneasiness lest the organization might become a haven for draft dodgers. There seemed to be an increasing number of healthy young men doing paper work that could and should be done by the older men first brought in for the purpose.

General Donovan acted with his usual vigor. He ordered the draft status of every individual male in the organization reviewed with the stipulation that there would be absolutely no deferments for anyone unless it could be proven beyond the slightest doubt that the service being performed was unique. It tightened things considerably but it also brought about some ludicrous situations. The Ph.D.s thought that they should all, if inducted into the service, have at least the rank of captain. It was a surprise to many that they settled for such lowly rank. Generals would have been more in keeping with their self-estimate. One eminent brain bucked for full commander in the Navy, had to settle for two-stripe lieutenant and was unpleased. Arguing that his two stripes had a tendency to downgrade the appraisal of his work with the services, he wangled permission to wear civilian clothes. He was naïve enough to find it difficult to understand why he could not receive his old civilian salary from OSS along with his new found Navy pay check.

One young man, fresh out of Harvard, and the son of a highly placed Government official, won a lieutenant junior grade commission out of the Navy. Then, when his father was sent into the European Theater on an assignment for the President, the son went along as Naval aide. With father holding ambassadorial rank, the London billeting was plush to say the least, but then a problem arose. The huge officers mess at Grosvenor House, called Willow Run, had a private dining room for full colonels and above. Father had a courtesy card but son, as a JG could not enter. So son obtained permission to wear civilian clothes on the assertion that the secrecy of his assignment demanded such "cover." Then, as a "high ranking" civilian, he happily obtained his coveted card and dined with the brass. This latter incident, fortunately, did not involve OSS personnel, although the son, for a very short period before his going into uniform, had been associated with the organization. General Donovan's comments on this type of abuse were salty and to the point, and his regard for persons involved in such maneuvers was nonexistent.

Although the pettiness of some of the members of R & A branch was appalling, it should not be assumed that the work of the branch was ineffective. Far from it. Painstaking hours of research turned out information exact in detail and of tremendous value in the mounting of espionage and sabotage operations. R & A reports furnished the background material for the original African landings, having furnished our services with every type of information from beach gradients and tidal currents in the landing area, to the placement and voltage of high tension electric installations. They were R & A estimates which pointed up the military potential of the Ploesti Oil fields and they were R & A maps which pinpointed the location of the prime targets in those fields for the subsequent air raids. R & A cartographers produced the largest globes ever made, one of which was sent to President Roosevelt for his use in the White House and the other of which was sent to Prime Minister Churchill to facilitate his following of the allied campaign.

It was an offshoot of R & A which produced one of the most fascinating of all products developed by OSS. This product was a highly ingenious explosive which we supplied to resistance groups behind enemy lines. It was made in the form of an ordinary flour and packaged in flour sacks. As such, it could quite safely be supplied to and stored by resistance families living quietly among the enemy. Should suspicious Germans question the innocent-looking "flour," the housewife involved could safely bake fresh bread or biscuits with the explosive powder. We called it our "Aunt Jemima" pancake flour.

R & A helped establish and staff the first Japanese language schools and furnished all of the background material on the Far Eastern cultures made available to our armed services. And when an agent finally went in to destroy a particular bridge it was an R & A report which had figured out for him how much and what type of explosive, where applied, would be most effective. Then, long before the final collapse of Germany, R & A reports were available on every country involved pointing up the economic, political, sociological, ethnic, psychological and geographic factors to be considered in peace settlements and post-war solutions and rehabilitation. They were in the President's portfolio in every major conference throughout the war and after, full, concise and detailed.

The Special Intelligence branch was the second major burden-bearer with respect to espionage operations. SI, as it was called, was headquartered in a temporary building down the hill from the R & A building. It was known as "Q," super-secret and super-select. Even regular investigated, trusted and tagged OSS personnel from the other branches had to sign in for an interview with anyone working in "Q" and free passage through the building was denied to all but a few, an escort-guard being the routine drill for anyone called in for conference.

David K. E. Bruce was the head of SI. A cosmopolitan in the very best sense of the word. David Bruce was intelligent, widely informed, travelled, sophisticated and urbane. It should be enough proof of his qualifications for the job to point out that, since his war service as a full colonel in charge of OSS operations in the European Theater, he has gone on in Government service to become, among other assignments, Secretary of Commerce, Ambassador to France, Ambassador to West Germany and is currently Ambassador to Great Britain. Allen Dulles, later to head the OSS operation in Switzerland and to serve as postwar head of the successor to OSS, the Central Intelligence Agency, was operating out of the New York office of SI.

It was up to David Bruce to build, from scratch, a tight, workable and, if possible, foolproof intelligence network. It made any other assignment within OSS look like a holiday if for no other reason than the fact that there is no book on how to develop such a network, there are no rules, other than the basic one of absolute security and no project can for a moment be considered complete and safe. Further, the intelligence gathered would be only as good as the preparation for the gathering of that intelligence. That meant time and work.

Special training schools had to be established where our agent candidates could be given the ultimate in preparation. All of the basics of spy fiction were there and more: the uses of special inks, photographic techniques, codes and secret entry; the establishment and maintenance of a "cover" story to erase real identity and create a new personality, an agent, real as life and yet basically phony. Nothing was overlooked.

Physical training experts hardened and muscled each agent to the perfection of a machine. Special teachers crammed them with the special knowledge necessary to each specific assignment. Psychologists twisted and taunted them, tested and retested in a search for the flaw that could mean the defeat of a mission. And all the while staff doctors stood by to test and check the physical stamina and condition.

Such schools were, ideally, located in a secluded area where maximum security could be maintained. And they were never restricted in curriculum to the extent that a new idea, a new course, a new technique could not be adopted, tested, and either incorporated or discarded. On the Donovan principle, nothing was impossible, nothing was too absurd to be disregarded. Everything was to be tested.

Gradually the net began to grow. From the pinpoint of

"Q" in Washington, the lines began to extend. To Morocco, to Algiers, to Tunisia, to Egypt. To Portugal, to Spain, to France and to Italy. To Greece, to Yugoslavia, to Turkey. To Norway, to Denmark and Sweden, Holland, Belgium, Poland and Switzerland. To Germany. To Russia. To Austria, Rumania and Czechoslovakia. The intelligence lines slithered and spread until OSS had an ear to the ground throughout all of the war areas and the contingent neutrals as well.

And as the reports began coming in, the lights burned all night long as the code clerks, the indispensable cryptographers, worked around the clock to decipher the mass of intelligence material. That, decoded, went on to the proper channel where it was made available to the service most capable of utilizing the particular information. Out of what still appeared to be chaos was coming the seed of success in a vast war effort.

If one could spot the Research and Analysis staffer by the thick glasses and library pallor so common to the group, one could spot the Special Intelligence staffer by the Ivy look. Just as General Donovan had recruited his friends, persons whom he knew personally and could vouch for, so the branch heads recruited those persons whom they could rely upon and trust beyond any doubt. It was only natural that David Bruce, having been tapped by Donovan for SI, should in turn recruit persons whom he had known personally for many years.

Himself a graduate of Princeton and a member of the Ivy club there, many of David Bruce's early recruits were Princeton and Ivy. Then, as the supply ran out, similar types from the other top universities and colleges came into the branch until the stamp had been made. As a result, the branch was responsible, more than any other section of OSS, for the smart cocktail-circuit quip in Washington, that OSS stood for Oh So Secret or Oh So Social. And then those in the know told off the names of some of the members: Bruce, Mellon, Vanderbilt, Morgan, Armour, Guest and Goddard. Such smart talk overlooked the basic fact that in each instance the person concerned was doing a full-time, productive and worthwhile job usually in an area for which no one had any advance training for the simple reason that none had previously existed.

It was SI which worked out the format for the infiltration of enemy territories. Each mission, with a pre-stated aim, was literally hand tailored to the job at hand. Even before an agent-volunteer had been tapped for assignment, the full detail of the mission was on paper, how it should be implemented, the full cover story, contacts, scope and duration. Then, with this in mind and an agent chosen for the job, the training was tailored along the lines to fit the mission. Every angle in the operation was checked and double-checked for security, efficiency and productivity until, insofar as possible, we could be sure that a successful mission was being mounted.

And a tremendous percentage of them were productive and successful. SI agents furnished material—intelligence data on troop concentrations and potentials, morale and the like—on which the Italian landings were based. They were SI agents who informed on the situation along the French Mediterranean Coast prior to the southern invasion. For months before D-Day OSS–SI agents were pouring a steady stream of vital information back to London from which the answer to almost any military, air or naval question could be found, involving enemy activity and capability.

It was an OSS agent who first tipped off our forces of the presence of General Rommel in the invasion area, a report which led to the General's ambush and injury a few days later. The location, number and fire-power of coastal defense installations in Norway? An OSS agent got the answer. Nazi plans for the use of displaced persons as double agents? An OSS agent produced the brief, and soon enough for us to take countermeasures. An attempt on Hitler's life? An OSS agent had the details back at headquarters before the general public in Germany knew the facts.

As the war progressed and the organization grew, General

Donovan insisted on more immediate service on the part of OSS to the armed services. Because of this, the point of emphasis shifted until the advance units of the organization were the major operating areas with Washington serving as a base headquarters. The OSS operation for the European Theater was based in London with the result that SI moved the greater part of its activity to the London base. This, of course, meant the establishment of new training schools for our agents, holding and rest areas and all of the related activities.

In this regard, originally established in Washington but only really in full flower in the war theaters, was established another branch called Special Operations or SO. Operating shoulder to shoulder with SI, SO was the branch responsible for the sabotage groups and the organization of the resistance groups in enemy territory. These were the boys who did the dirty work, the demolitions, the assassinations, the harassments and the equipping of resistance fighters and partisans.

Here again, special schools and training areas had to be established for the teaching of sabotage techniques. Fortunately, in the European Theater, OSS was able to work closely with the British in this regard and, to a great extent, to share some of their training areas. The British commando schools were rugged proving grounds for sabotage agents where the toughest possible training was imposed. Nothing was spared, proof being that, when a big installation was the target of a sabotage operation a full scale mock-up of the project was built on which the trainees could practice. The classic example of this type of training is the one, already well known, of the scale replica made of the cliffs and streets of Dieppe on which the commandos trained for their ill-fated raid.

SO operations were the thriller operations usually associated in the public mind with OSS. They were closest to the fiction-type exploits in which all is action, danger and death. In actual fact, though they were of course hazardous missions as are all operations behind enemy lines, many of the most successful sabotage operations were quiet, long drawn out programs of petty harassment or the tedious, nerve-tensing, day-in-day-out buildup of a strong resistance striking force.

It would be almost impossible to list the successful sabotage and resistance-organized operations of OSS. They were numerous and constant. They operated throughout North Africa. They fought isolated small wars in the rugged mountains of Italy, Yugoslavia and Greece, most of them so remote and small as to have escaped attention in the larger panorama of the war, and yet, by their very terror and nuisance value, by their hit-and-run techniques, a major factor in the defeat of the Axis. They blanketed France with their boldness and, as we have seen with Duval, they organized not only small, but full-scale, effective regiments of resistance, ready and able to strike with crippling force when the time was right. They spread like a plague through Norway, Denmark and the Low Countries, burning, exploding, sinking, demolishing and killing whenever and wherever their blows could be most telling.

Many of the sabotage agents operated alone, some went in teams of two or three and many, in cooperation with the Special Intelligence branch, went in with an espionage agent and a radio operator. Everything was tried, all variations were assessed and utilized; it all depended on the particular objective at hand.

A later development, as the fad for psychological warfare grew in importance, a third operational branch was established called Morale Operations or MO, for short. It was the function of MO to deal in black propaganda in an effort to undermine the morale of enemy troops and the population generally.

The one glory of MO was the establishment of a super-powerful radio station on the continent shortly after D-Day. Known as *Soldatensender Calais,* the station was beamed at German troops with an insidious programming of morale-breaking material. It was a clever operation. A typical soldier-oriented type

83

of program, most of the day was filled with music, chitchat and news. The music was nostalgic with the aim of promoting and spreading homesickness through the troops. The chitchat was mostly innocuous but with a subtly placed barb of satire or criticism aimed to fester and grow within the listener's mind. The news was the real core of the operation. Carefully, factually, truthfully, news items which could be verified by the enemy troops were broadcast to them to gain their confidence. Two days, three days, of straight news items would be fed the troops. Then, when their faith in the accuracy of the reports had been established, a black propaganda item would be inserted. A spate of successes would be followed by a black item to the effect that a super-secret top level conference of all the high officers of the Wehrmacht was being held in Berlin, indicative, perhaps, of serious trouble ahead for the Nazis. Another two or three days of straight reporting and then another suggestion of trouble, the sudden suicide of a top general, perhaps, or the failure of a much boasted super-weapon.

Doubt, dissatisfaction, distrust and more, the spreading of these morale-destroying elements occupied the MO staffers to the exclusion of everything else. And yet, of all OSS operations, the effectiveness of MO would be the most difficult to assess. It was almost impossible to determine how many defections there were in the German ranks as the war progressed. It would be even more difficult to pinpoint how many of those defections could be attributed to the eroding effect of *Soldatensender Calais*. However, the lack of an assessment or any means for an assessment in no way slackened the effort. Win, lose, or draw, the black propaganda of MO was disseminated throughout the enemy ranks as a constant threat to the solidity of the German front.

Like the growing giant that it was, the pulsing expansion of OSS called again and constantly for new assignments, new bases, changes in command and all the rest.

David Bruce, now a full colonel, had been lifted out of SI by General Donovan and made commanding officer of the OSS operation in the European Theater. As such, he was responsible for all OSS operations of whatever kind from Norway to Italy, a job for which he was eminently well prepared. For that purpose, OSS had established a forward headquarters in London from which all continental operations would be mounted.

It began surreptitiously as an adjunct of the American Embassy in London and, for all outward purposes, personnel of OSS were accredited to the Embassy as State Department employees. At best it was a makeshift arrangement, capable of operation only so long as the OSS staff remained small. But so vast and far reaching were the Donovan plans, so complex and super-secret were the OSS missions, it soon became evident that it would be forced to go its own way, divorced from the Embassy and independently housed. Seventy-two Grosvenor Street was the original address under this new independent setup. It later overflowed to 70, then 68 and finally to innumerable other buildings scattered about London, exclusive of the training areas, holding areas and rest houses maintained in the country.

By now my own career with OSS had catapulted me overseas and into the London office. I had immensely enjoyed working with the Research and Analysis branch but I also longed to get more actively into the war with overseas service if possible. I had indicated my interest in active service in several discussions with Commander Vanderbilt and General Donovan.

Several factors played into my hands. One, the emphasis was now shifting to the overseas operations with the attendant problems of personnel, administration and the like. Secondly, the Special Funds branch, the secret banking operation necessary to the financing of the agent operations on the continent, was finding its original operating plan unworkable. In the early days, Special Funds simply made each agent operator in effect a representative of Special Funds with direct accountability.

But as the numbers grew, a hopeless tangle of representatives with only the vaguest knowledge of the intricacies of agent financing began to develop. Obviously, the answer was to have a Special Funds representative at the forward London base to whom all agents and agent operators would be responsible. General Donovan and Commander Vanderbilt, in conversations with Colonel Lane Rehm, head of the whole Special Funds organization and with the concurrence of Colonel Bruce, decided that I should be that man. With a captain's commission in the Army of the United States, I was assigned to the London office as Administrative-Executive Officer to Colonel Bruce and as Special Funds officer for OSS in the European Theater. In view of the fact that I found the balancing of my own checkbook a monumental challenge, the latter assignment was, to me, numbing in its implications. General Donovan eased the burden considerably by one of his parting comments before I left for London.

"Cheer up, Bob," he said. "We'll find plenty of people to add and subtract the figures for you. The main thing is that we want you, in whom we have confidence, to handle the problem."

No one less military ever wore uniform. I got through a required OSS course of training on how to handle arms, how to wear, and function in a gas mask and related items. But I was never sure I could have hit anything with any kind of weapon.

Though it may be an incidental and unimportant digression, my crossing to England was memorable. I was on orders with a full Colonel which was great luck because, with his rank, he was entitled to relative privacy. We shared what had been a single cabin on the Queen Elizabeth. She was painted in her wartime grey, low in the water because of the tremendous load she was expected to carry, and was barely able to clear the top of the Holland Tunnel going down river at high tide. I had not met my travelling cabin mate prior to the crossing so my first view of him was on finding my way to the stateroom we were to share.

He was in the lower berth when I walked in, although it was late afternoon. I introduced myself and received as acknowledgement only the blinking of tiny, unfocusing eyes which seemed lost against the promontory of a large, very round and brilliant red nose. There was some sparse, sandy red hair and a short red moustache on a smallish head. All else was bedding. However, on the floor, well within reach, was a half-emptied bottle of scotch.

The Queen Elizabeth, like her sister ship the Queen Mary, crossed the Atlantic as a troop transport alone, without benefit of convoy, relying on her speed to save her from the lurking wolf packs of the Nazi submarines. No one knows our course but it was obviously erratic from the fact that one day would be freezing cold and the next hot and humid. And besides, one had only to watch the crazy zigzag pattern of our wake to know that this was no ordinary crossing. We were four days, however, and not without incident, to Gourock, Scotland. And not once in those four days did I see my Colonel out of his bed. No matter when or how often I returned to our cabin, the two beady eyes were staring at me, the bulbous red nose sat on the edge of the covers like a child's rubber ball and the stack of empty whiskey bottles grew and grew.

The Colonel was a retread from the first World War. It was a surprise to me, on reaching Scotland, to discover that he had been named as commandant of the troop train carrying us to London. It was an even greater surprise to learn that he had appointed me as his adjutant for the journey. Since we had exchanged not more than two dozen words in the four-day crossing I wondered how he had come to the decision. Worse, I wondered how he would be able to rise from his bed, dress and make it to the train.

His arrival was something to see. We were in a war zone and he had obviously decided to acknowledge that fact. He was wearing full battle dress, combat boots, side arms buckled over his tunic, gas mask slung over his shoulder and steel helmet.

The helmet was oversize for his small head with the result that he had the slightly ridiculous appearance of a small boy impersonating a man. Even the small red moustache helped that illusion with the impression of having been pasted on under the rubber-ball nose. In view of the fact that we were in Northern Scotland and about as far from any war front as it would be possible to get in the British Isles, his costume was, to say the least, overstressed.

Somehow the vast contingent of troops packed into the special troop trains and we set out for London. It was a long, tedious trip but it was relieved three times by stops of fifteen or twenty minutes. At each stop, neatly tailored women of the British Red Cross were on hand with steaming tea, coffee, doughnuts and cigarettes. And at each stop our Colonel, as train commandant, descended to receive the ladies and thank them for their kindness. He stepped rather stiffly from the train each time, walked slowly toward the head Red Cross lady and, to the amazement of all concerned, instead of proffering a hand or flipping a salute, he would slowly, stiffly bend at the waist until his body was in a right angle bow. The lady receiving such attention got to see only the top of a steel helmet, which was perhaps just as well.

Our ways parted on arrival in London and I only saw the Colonel a couple of times after that. Each time he was walking stiffly, peering through tiny, unsteady eyes around his red bulbous nose. Then, later on, I heard that he had died suddenly of cirrhosis of the liver in a hospital and had been buried in a military cemetery in England.

The "characters" were still with us. And I must say it was more of a shock to find them in London than it had been to see them in Washington. It's not that we had so many of them but rather that, in view of the tremendous screening processes which had been developed, we had any at all.

There was another "desk snob." This time it was a full Colonel and a West Point product who went off and bought himself an elegantly carved antique desk because, as he stated quite blandly, "I am dealing with many British, French and other allied Generals and Admirals and the setting should be appropriate." It apparently never occurred to him that Colonel Bruce, his commanding officer and head of the outfit, seemed to find a more modest desk perfectly adequate.

There was the retired professor who insisted that his crucial work with our organization and relations with the Eighth Air Force should necessitate a personal car and chauffeur. It was, he felt, beneath his station to be forced to use the cars from the motor pool and anyway, he had, once or twice, had to wait a few minutes for one to be available. When the matter was discussed with him further, it was discovered that he quite seriously thought that OSS should provide him with a Rolls Royce limousine and liveried chauffeur. With considerable pettishness he finally settled for a baby Austin to drive himself. He was the only person in the organization so equipped.

The most astonishing bit of conceit involved a branch chief who decided to decamp from Washington to run his organization from the London base. As the only over-all branch head directing his work from London he felt himself rather special. How special had not been guessed until the gentleman required additional space for his unit. A complete, rather elegant London town house was requisitioned for him. The main drawing rooms were richly panelled, there was a small private garden and terrace, and the four floors of the house provided many and varied rooms for his personnel. The whole was redone to his requirements with full telephone service to each room, security controls and the like.

When the building was finally ready, more complete and certainly more elaborate than anything OSS had produced for its personnel elsewhere in London, the branch was moved in, the presiding chief was installed in his private offices and his approval of the premises sought. He gave his reaction in two words.

Asked how he liked the setup, his reply was "It stinks." He then went on to outline the importance of his position. And while his listeners stood disbelieving, he explained how he was not only the head of the branch in London, as were others here, but that he was head of the whole branch operation, "here, Washington, throughout the world. I am the head of this branch, Universe."

General Donovan's comment was that he was a "pompous little ass but effective in his job." So he was tolerated.

It was a fascinating study in human nature, the London OSS operation. Here were men prominent, cultivated, rich, seeking only to do a job well and unobtrusively, accepting any and all inconveniences of war without complaint, rather almost gladly as one more thing they could do to help. And on the other hand were a few who never before had held so much power, had such prestige or so much money to spend and showed it by pomposity, self-importance, rudeness and jealousy. Here Capt. Junius Spencer Morgan, USN, scion of the house of Morgan, saw no reason why he shouldn't squat on the floor of a locked office at midnight to count gold Louis d'Or from sacks leg-chained to an OSS courier. And there, a self-centered little man was demanding a private house for his own use.

One so often hears the cliché that the truly great are always simple. It is a cliché because it is true and, under the stress of war and the tension of secret operations, its truth stood out embarrassingly in OSS. Here we had hundreds of dedicated people working without thought of self or time, urged on by a drive to be ever more effective regardless of the personal sacrifice involved. In appalling contrast was the officer who flew his French mistress, dressed as a WAC, to London for a week end, shortly after the liberation of Paris.

90

At the London end, both SI and SO were operating in close conjunction with their complementary British services. The exchange of ideas, plans and facilities was real, although it goes without saying that we certainly never told the British everything any more than they let us in on their most secret plans and thoughts. Likewise, there was close work with the Free French and the Poles, Belgians, Norwegians, Danes and Dutch with respect to both intelligence and sabotage operations.

Apart from these two operating branches, a third intelligence branch was now functioning in a highly specialized area. Labelled X2 and headed by Jimmy Murphy, a slight, sandy-haired Irishman who had started his career in the organization as secretary to General Donovan, it was charged with the problem of counterintelligence. This was the real nightmare realm of operation, where one got to the point of not being able to believe his own grandmother, so suspicious did one become. It was up to X2 to discover and utilize the services of enemy agents but always aware that a double agent may very possibly become the most unreliable of all sources, a double-double agent.

X2 operated from London in a building at some distance from the regular OSS headquarters and later, after D-Day and the liberation of Paris, from an independent location in Paris. Any defecting enemy personnel, a "blown" enemy agent, the most cynical of international mercenaries, all were potentials for X2. And if ever there was any doubt about the security and reliability of one of our regular agents, it was X2 that stepped in to settle the issue.

The real field day came for X2 after D-Day. Then, with refugees, escapees, ex-forced labor types and the like with which the continent was flooded, X2 had fertile fields in which to operate. It made the most of them. And, along with the SI and SO missions, made OSS an extremely productive and sophisticated intelligence operation.

General Donovan's vision had paid off. From the early days of the Office of Coordinator of Information in 1941, to the war-proven efficiency of the Office of Strategic Services in 1945 had been a giant step. It had been made because one man visualized the need for every type of specialist, every type of knowledge, every type of idea brought together under one unit and directed toward one goal. Every part fitted every other part in a dependent and interrelated net so complicated that it could almost be said that the quiet little man with the thick glasses sitting in Washington verifying some metric gauge was as important as the secret agent lying quietly in the midst of enemy territory sending back information. Specialized knowledge was found in strange places and often sheer coincidence proved valuable in the solution of a problem.

One classic story involved the bird problem on Ascension Island. An emergency base established on Ascension Island by the Air Force found itself plagued with the persistence of a particularly large flock of sea birds. For generations, apparently, Ascension had been the breeding and nesting area for these flocks and the mere fact that a war had brought men and machines to their roosts in no way dissuaded them from returning. Each take-off and landing at Ascension was a supreme hazard because of the circling flocks disturbed by the planes. Every effort of the Air Force to dislodge the birds permanently had failed.

OSS had on its staff several noted ornithologists. They were with us, not because we were primarily interested in birds but because, in their careers as ornithologists, they had become familiar with some of the most remote and inaccessible areas of the world. General Donovan felt that we might like to know more about these areas, so the gentlemen in question were taken into OSS where their knowledge proved of tremendous practical value. It so happened that one of these men, while on a flight to Europe, made an emergency landing at Ascension. His natural interest in the birds led the base commandant to tell of his problem. Our ornithologist solved it for him quite simply. All that would be necessary, he explained, would be for the commandant to spread chicken wire of a gauge large enough to let the eggs drop through some few feet above the ground. Once the birds found that each egg was broken in its fall as it was laid they would abandon the site. And that is exactly what happened.

CHAPTER 6

EPISODES AND CHARACTERS

PERHAPS the greatest single asset of OSS as an organization was its ability and willingness to exploit every opportunity no matter how difficult or strange it might be. At the very outbreak of the war one of the first projects undertaken by the agency was the screening of tourists from overseas and the utilizing of thousands of their photographs taken abroad. Certainly in the first days of the war it must have puzzled more than one citizen to have the U.S. Government suddenly show great interest in the picture of Aunt Minnie taken at Toulon, or the photograph of Uncle George in Tunisia, or the one that Johnnie had sent back from Tokyo. It might now satisfy their curiosity to know that from just such photographs OSS was able to gain highly valuable and up-dated information on the French naval base which just happened to be the background for Aunt Minnie, that Uncle George was standing within range of a large refinery in Tunisia; and that Johnnie had a pretty good shot of a recent electrical installation in Japan. At first glance it seemed like a ridiculous idea. The results more than made up for the time and effort involved in screening thousands of photographs.

From such photographs invaluable information was extracted with the aid of magnifying glasses, blow-ups of important details were made and a tremendous file of pertinent data made available to back up and to pinpoint intelligence and sabotage projects.

Another similarly exhaustive reference file was built up on personalities. Germans, French, Italians first, and then key people in every facet of life in every country in any way involved in the war were grist to the OSS mill. A quick run-down of this file would tell you the whole story on any individual: his position, official or private; financial status, rich or poor, inherited or self-made wealth; social position; marital status and family connections, with emphasis on any foreign connections; political affiliations and stability; personal traits, whether sportive, intellectual, social or not; weaknesses such as women, drink or gambling; integrity and the like; in fact anything at all that might be of value in determining the person's value to OSS and the Allied cause.

It was from this file that we obtained some of our most valued workers, our couriers. These people are not to be confused with the regular couriers, those security messengers who were entrusted with seeing that top secret documents were conveyed directly from person to person no matter how great the distance, or how difficult the delivery problem. OSS employed many young men as regular couriers to do this work.

But there was another, more important type of courier, whose name never appeared on any OSS roster, who never received any remuneration for services rendered, in fact who seldom had direct contact with any bona fide OSS employee or agent. This type of courier was a person whose entire background and sympathies were known and beyond question, with the added advantage of being resident in enemy-occupied territory. Such a person was able to carry messages, either verbal or written, usually the former, between two agents who wished to conceal their contact. The messages were invariably of no meaning whatsoever to the courier involved, so that there was no danger of any security leak and yet the link was vital as a cut-out, the go-between that protected the identity and operating safety of the agents concerned.

One of the really amusing incidents to come out of the war concerned just such a courier.

Our personality file had revealed, quite naturally, many Americans living abroad, particularly in France. For the most part these expatriates had returned to the United States at the outbreak of war but a few had stayed on. One was an American woman living in France. Shortly after the first World War she had married a Frenchman and had lived almost continuously in France with only occasional trips to America. She and her husband maintained a small apartment in Paris which they used infrequently, but they spent most of each year on a country estate which had been in the family for generations. Madame had so completely fitted in to the French way of life over the years, she was regarded by the natives in the surrounding countryside as one of them. It was a natural for OSS.

When the Second World War broke out Madame was a widow, childless, nearing seventy, and living quietly in her small chateau in the French countryside. It never occurred to her to abandon France and return to America to sit out the war. OSS made contact with her and asked if she would be willing to act as a courier for us. It was not a demanding assignment for an elderly woman but it did call for discretion, intelligence and nerve. It meant that, on occasion and after proper identification through prearranged code, she would be asked to transmit messages for our operatives.

Madame agreed to work for us and she became an extremely valuable link in one of our chains. Over a period of many months she was called upon to act as a cut-out and she was always effective, discreet and successful. But her career was not without its excitement.

One sultry summer day Madame decided to go into Paris by train on purely personal business. It was most definitely fortunate, in view of what happened, that she was not at the time involved in any specific mission for OSS.

During the journey on a hot, sticky and crowded train, Madame found it necessary to go to the lavatory. At the best of times the toilets on French trains leave a great deal to be desired. In war-time France they were appalling. Madame very carefully spread her morning newspaper over the toilet seat before using it and remarked to herself on her good fortune in having it with her for the purpose.

Shortly after Madame had returned to her compartment the train was brought to an abrupt halt at a small station. There were loud voices and many German soldiers on the platform and soon there were Germans going through the train asking for identity cards. Everyone was checked. But, the passengers shrugged, this was one of the inconveniences of war, especially in an occupied country. They sat in the stifling heat and waited.

Now, suddenly, there were shouted orders, much confusion and everyone was ordered from the train and into the station. Someone suggested that perhaps the Germans were searching for some particular person as this was unusual. The next moment they were segregated, the men sent into one room, the women crowded into another.

A tall, rather bloated and red-faced German woman in Nazi uniform came in and ordered all of the women to strip to the skin. A slight hesitation brought a sharp yelp of command from the German woman and the passengers began to remove

97

their clothes. Madame slipped off her dress, her slip, her under-garments. She hesitated at her shoes and stockings but was told everything must come off, everything!

Two more German women in uniform had now come into the small and stifling room, grotesque with the fading shapes of nude French country women. They were shaking clothing, probing bodies, moving arrogantly among the embarrassed nudes. They came to Madame, riffled through her clothing, made her take down her hair, turned her around.

One of the Germans made a sudden, explosive sound, spoke to the others and, with one swift motion, bent Madame double. There were shouts of triumph from the three Germans and one was dispatched immediately. After some minutes she returned bearing a fly-specked mirror from the washroom.

Madame was pushed across a table and, to her horror and yet secret amusement, waited while the three German women attempted to read what apparently was the morning's news from her bare behind. In vain she protested that, if there was any-thing printed on her flesh, it had come about quite innocently because she had utilized the newspaper as a sanitary precau-tion in the toilet. She tried to explain that obviously the mois-ture of her warm flesh had picked up the ink from the inferior newsprint but the more she explained, the more logical it sounded, the more convinced were the Germans that they had discovered a spy and an ingenious method of communication. Even the obvious news item character of the writing only con-vinced them that it was all part of the code.

They had to work hard for their information. The print was of course inverted so that every word had to be reflected in the mirror and then translated. But it did not deter them. Letter by letter, word by word, with occasional gaps where the impres-sion was not clear, the three German women copied the news from Madame's behind. An hour later they allowed her to straighten up.

There was a further delay, during which time two of the
98

three German women were out of the room, apparently in conference with their commandant. At last they returned, barked orders for the unfortunate passengers to dress and get back in the train.

The rest of the trip into Paris was without incident.

As Madame told her story to us in Paris after the liberation, General Donovan laughed as I had never seen him laugh before. It was the person of Madame that gave the story its wildly incongruous humor. Here was a woman, *soignée* as the French would say, elegant, aristocratic. As she sat there telling her story she could have been the dowager matriarch of a very important family, carefully nurtured, genteely educated, always correct, modest. The picture of her in so ridiculous and immodest a situation was something straight out of a slapstick film.

To her great credit she saw the whole hilarious picture herself and laughed with us until she cried.

"I gave my all for my country," she commented laughingly.

"Or to be trite," added General Donovan, "service over and above the call of duty."

War has always been incongruous, placing the glory often on undeserving shoulders, overlooking or even ignoring the real heroes. We all know the Legion commanders who never saw active service. We all know of Generals living on retirement pay with medical benefits who never got out of a desk chair outside the country and yet ride at the head of a Memorial Day parade in an open car. We never hear of the GI who threw himself on a grenade to save his buddy, because they were both killed. We never hear of the secret agents who lived days and weeks of hell to produce one tiny item of information vital to a military plan. We know they were there and yet we shrug them off.

It would be impossible to try to relate all of the exciting, dangerous and heroic missions performed by secret agents in

99

the Second World War. And in most instances the key agent himself would be the first to deprecate his part, insisting that to a great extent his success as an agent was dependent on dozens of dedicated, hard working people behind him insuring the security and support of his mission. But the fact remains that the agent in the field, the man or woman operating alone or with a few others in enemy territory, is bearing the brunt of the effort and is displaying reservoirs of skill and courage seldom found in the average individual. When one bears in mind the fact that, if caught, his very existence is denied by the organization for which he works, one may have some slight grasp of the nerve such work demands.

There was the team of two agents which produced a steady stream of vital information from the very midst of German military activity in France. It was immediate and accurate information but it was obtained with great daring and imagination.

In almost any part of France and particularly in the country towns, there are vendors of local wines who utilize huge wooden casks to transport their product. The casks, many of which are in the proportion of hogsheads, are usually mounted on a two-wheeled cart chassis. There is a short pair of shaft-like pulls with a cross bar for hauling. The vendors push these casks through the town and sell direct to the local customers by simply drawing the required amount of wine from a bung hole at the bottom of the cask.

Our resourceful agents decided to make use of the innocent mobility of one of these casks. They built a dividing partition into one of the larger casks so that the bottom half could still be filled with wine but leaving the upper portion dry and usable for their purpose. In the upper half they installed a short-wave transmitter. Very cleverly they formed a lid in the upper portion of the cask by following the lines of the staves and hiding all fasteners on the inside. Then, when all was ready, the radio operator climbed into the upper portion of the cask with his set, fastened his lid into position so that it could not be opened from the outside, and was ready to function. His teammate, with the bottom half of the cask filled with wine, was free to patrol the streets of the area in search of the most important German activity of the moment. They had worked out every detail.

While waiting for customers the peddlar advised his hidden teammate of what was going on that might be of interest to our intelligence units in London. The radio operator, waiting until the cask was in motion, encoded his message. Then, when the teammate pushed his cask to another location, the transmitter went into operation sending out the pertinent data. In this way any German attempt at D-F-ing, the direction-finding techniques whereby they uncovered and pinpointed clandestine radio transmitters, was made not only difficult but nearly impossible. It was perfectly simple for the teammate on the outside to spot telltale radio D-F-ing trucks as they cruised the area. And once spotted, all he had to do was to remain in his chosen location as it was understood that the radio operator would transmit only when the cask was actually in motion.

This team operated almost daily for months without detection. They sent back to OSS headquarters in London information on the movement of German troops and armor. They told us the strength of the divisions, who was in command, what type of equipment they had, their physical condition and morale. They pinpointed supply dumps and lines of communication for our bombers to deal with. They located command posts for the same purpose. They observed the French populace and judged their readiness for organization into resistance groups. And later, when it was decided to send resistance organizers and saboteurs into the area, they were the ones who set up the drop area for us, manned it with reliable resistance workers from the area and insured the initial success of the mission.

It was tedious, nerve-wracking, dangerous business. It had

none of the glamour usually associated with espionage. It had nothing to do with champagne parties with a blonde under romantic conditions. The really productive espionage operations rarely do except in films. It had none of the exhilaration of battle, none of the camaraderie of troop action which helps to keep a man going in war. It was a lonely, hazardous ordeal where every moment called for alertness and caution.

It was the essence of heroism.

We had another operative who boasted that he spent most of the war in bed, flat on his back. And with incredible self-effacement he has used that simple statement on more than one occasion to parry any probing questions into what he did during the war.

The statement is quite true. He did spend several weeks flat on his back in bed. It was the most productive period of his entire mission, a project which, with great imagination, he had developed himself.

One of the strongest unions in all of France is that which protects and binds together the concierges, those portal guardians of practically every building in the country. Furnished with a small apartment just inside the main door of every apartment house and office building, the concierge is, I suppose we would say, a glorified janitor with status. He, or more often she, guards the doorway, literally. With an electric control, if modernized, or manually, she answers the doorbell and opens the huge doors which keep the public out of most French buildings. She handles the mail, takes messages, observes all comings and goings and wields considerable power. How much power may be understood when one realizes that, even after the German occupation, the concierges were left guarding the doors of France even in those buildings which had been requisitioned by the German Government for their uses.

The Luftwaffe had taken over one of the large office buildings in Paris for a headquarters. And the concierge who had sat in the little glassed box inside the doorway before the outbreak of war still sat there under the German occupation. Our agent made contact.

He had fantastic luck. Under the very noses of the Germans the concierge and her husband had been, not actively, in the resistance, but in a position to help their compatriots and to observe the German activity. Our man came to them with a plan and they agreed to work with him to the extent of giving him a base from which to operate and a cover for his mission.

With his forged documents all in order he made direct contact with the officer in charge of the building, a German of rank who passed on everything to do with the running of the office. His story was that he had come into Paris for shelter with the concierge and his wife, his only "relatives," because his own house had been bombed out by the RAF. Would it be permissible, since the concierge and his wife were agreeable, for him to stay with them for a while? He would, of course, be working by day as his work card showed. The unsuspecting German officer had no objection.

Our agent moved in. The concierge's apartment was of three small rooms, a combination kitchen–dining room with the inevitable glass window into the hall of the building and the lace curtains common to the concierge establishment, a small sitting room and a bedroom. For the first few days he was careful to leave each morning and return each night as one regularly employed. The Germans in the building ignored his presence.

Then, when he had everything in readiness, he took to his bed. "La grippe," the concierge told everyone, had taken hold of his "cousin" and he was confined to his bed. It was a singularly satisfactory illness.

Our agent had been able to install one of our small induction microphones in the building running into the very heart

103

of the Paris operation of the Luftwaffe command. The hair-like wire from the delicate instrument which could pick up conversation through a wall or through phone wires without direct tapping procedures trailed down to his bed in the concierge's quarters. There, under the covers of his bed, he had a tiny radio short-wave transmitter.

All day long he lay in his bed listening to the most secret of the Luftwaffe's conversations and plans. Their estimates of our D-Day strength and the punch necessary to counter it. He got them. The Germans' own estimates of their plane losses. He got them. The Allied destruction of German targets, the estimates of German fuel supplies for their planes, the reassignment of German squadrons. He got them all. The first signs of panic, the first official admission of German weakness in the air, the first recognition of Allied air superiority, those too he got.

And late at night, when the time seemed safe, he short-waved the information back to London from his "sick bed." However, that part of the operation was highly risky in Paris with the constant German vigilance for clandestine transmitters. Our man recognized that fact and was smart enough to realize that the information he was obtaining was too important, his listening post too vital to be lost through the hazard of direct transmission of his information. He was discreet enough and realistic enough to discontinue his own transmission. He made arrangements to relay his information to another operator who could send more freely.

It was a tremendously successful mission. From just prior to D-Day until after the liberation of Paris, in other words from late May of 1944 until late August, our man lay a-bed in the concierge's bedroom in Paris supplying us with highly vital information. It was information from the very heart of the German air effort against our invasion forces, intelligence of the highest priority and of tremendous value to our war effort. It was accomplished with great daring, with vision, with

104

cunning and with assurance. The concierge and his wife went about their daily chores with a boredom and calm which made his position relatively safe and secure. Our man insisted that the Germans had even forgotten he existed. It would have been nice to think so!

There was just one final bit of bravado to the mission. Just to prove that all of his time was not spent in bed our man brought me a souvenir. It is a Luftwaffe target map of London and the Thames estuary.

All of the bravery was not confined to men within the OSS. Many young women operated for us in assignments of tremendous importance and great danger. In every instance they showed steel-nerved calm, resourcefulness and cunning, whether they were involved in straight espionage, as were most, or in the more rigorous program of organizing resistance and directing sabotage.

A young Italian girl performed exceptional feats in the organization and sustenance of the partisan groups in northern Italy. And she was not alone. There were countless others throughout the length of Italy who fought silently and tirelessly to aid the Allied cause. In France the same pattern was repeated from the example of the young French girl who calmly stood at a crossroads and misdirected a retreating German Army into an Allied trap, to the young American woman who smuggled sabotage equipment to resistance groups.

One of our best female operatives was a young American woman of strapping physique. She was strong, husky and athletic beyond the average; she knew the continent well and was fluent in both French and German. She dropped into France on two different occasions for us and performed effectively and with distinction. She made only one concession to the whole operation. Just before parachuting into enemy territory she insisted on a man-sized slug of brandy. She had it so well-organized she knew just how much to take to give her the added courage to go in without going over the edge and dulling her perception to the danger point. It was all very simple, no brandy, no drop.

It is remarkable that the women were not limited to the espionage type of operation but proved equally effective in the tougher, rougher sabotage and guerrilla assignments. Perhaps our outstanding woman operative, certainly our most daring, chose to function in this field. Slight of figure, wiry, taller than average, soft-spoken, quiet and unassuming, she would be the last person one would believe to be suitable agent material. She was, in fact, superb.

She had been dropped into occupied France once for a specific assignment, completed her mission and been brought back out for rest and retraining. Then, in March, 1944, she was parachuted again into occupied France for work with the French underground and resistance groups. Although in her earlier mission she had had a brush with the Gestapo and was known as an OSS agent she immediately established radio contact with London headquarters and again began supplying a steady stream of intelligence and operational information. Then, in cooperation with a Jedburgh team of American and British organizers and saboteurs, she began to organize, train and equip resistance groups. Throughout her mission she was hunted by the Gestapo and, even though she was operating in an area of intensive German military activity, she maintained a cool, calm determination to succeed.

That she did. For through the efforts of this girl three full battalions of French resistance forces were put into the field for the harassment of enemy troops and installations. They cut communications, destroyed supplies and materiel, and demoralized troops. And even though she at times had to hide for her life, the work that she had so courageously implemented went on.

Throughout all of her work for OSS this young woman asked for only one special consideration. It seems she had a wooden leg and she insisted that she be permitted to parachute with her wooden leg tucked under her arm in order to be sure that it would not be broken in the landing. The request was granted. In this manner her drops were made, the wooden leg arrived in France intact and her missions were accomplished.

She caused us some concern after the liberation of Paris because several days passed before she made contact with our quickly established headquarters. When she finally did appear she had with her only the clothes on her back and explained, rather apologetically, that she had been forced to hide out for a while from the Gestapo or she would have checked in earlier. One might have thought she was apologizing for having missed a train connection and deplored the inconvenience it might have caused those waiting for her.

The importance of her mission? It was officially recognized by the United States Government after the war with the award of the Distinguished Service Cross. I believe she was the first woman so honored by our country for heroism in war.

Meanwhile, incredible as it may seem, an occasional sour apple was still able to appear on the scene in London. Invariably these personalities had come into the organization with high promise but because of some lack of dedicated drive or a failure to submerge themselves in the anonymity of an operation such as OSS demanded, they became rootless within the organization. Often, because Washington could not use them and found them increasingly in the way, they were sent overseas as a sop to their self-esteem and in an effort to shift the burden of responsibility for their useful employment.

One such individual drifted through the London office for several months desperately trying to create, anywhere, somewhere, a position which he deemed worthy of himself. He insisted that he should operate only at the very highest level. A civilian, he plagued both OSS and the Embassy in London, with requests for special favors. He asked for a simulated rank and thought it should be that of brigadier-general. In view of the fact that this brought him alongside of General Donovan and above Colonel Bruce, it was indeed strange that he could not see the conceit in his request. It was not granted. He wrote countless memos asking for passes to the General's mess, permission to sit in on high level command meetings, permission to "observe" war at first hand by being flown to the front and given a personal tour of the battle fields. He even sought access to all high level command files of the Allied forces! And when all of these requests were denied with cool logic in view of the fact that his interest seemed to be more that of a personal busybody than a productive worker, he petulantly complained that the effect of such denial on his standing and reputation back at his university would be irreparable. He put that in writing!

To those of us who daily saw more and more fearless, selfless individuals launched on missions of the highest danger, it was sickening to have to waste as much as a moment in consideration of the professor's prestige problems.

There was another one of those "quick change" artists who appeared briefly in London, the type who bucked for a commission because he felt he could be "more effective" in uniform and then, when the commission came through with a rank disappointingly lower than he thought he deserved, turned around and sought permission to wear civilian clothes "because the delicate nature of his assignment demanded mufti." He it was who thought OSS should supply its agents with unmounted diamonds to be used as an escape item, in case of capture. As an item of small size and great value, he argued, an agent could carry two or three secreted in the rectum. One wag observed that in case of capture by the enemy anything hidden in the rectum would no doubt be one of the first things lost. And although all of our operatives had found that the usual method of agent financing with solid currency was by far the most effective, this individual insisted that his men be provided with diamonds for their rectums. These, he insisted, would be used only in case of capture, to be bribes for escape. It was interesting to observe that almost every one of his returning agents reported the stones as "lost." The more cynical among our staff felt they must have been lost in houses of pleasure. Not one ever was reported as having been used in escape.

Still another over-eager amateur nearly brought on a full-scale diplomatic-military crisis in his enthusiasm. He was working with a foreign group, one of that great mass of alien nationals of countries under the Nazi heel, interested in an organized effort to recapture their countries. These foreign nationals, as members of their own military services, were on the military payroll of their own governments in exile. Our boy was much disturbed by the low pay scale of these men and decided to do something about it. Quite on his own, without consultation with any responsible party in the OSS, he undertook to promise the alien nationals working with him that our organization would give them a supplemental salary over and above their regular army pay from their own government.

OSS did, as an accepted and regular practice, add a so-called "agent's pay" to the base pay and allowances of any GI operating on an actual espionage or sabotage mission. But for the period prior to the mission, when an agent was in training, his pay was purely an army matter. In this particular misunderstanding the foreign nationals had been led to believe that they would be placed on a supplemental OSS payroll as soon as they signed up for training. When, for obvious reasons, it was explained to them that no arm of the U.S. Government could be meddling in the pay scales of a foreign government, we had a small scale mutiny on our hands.

When agent morale vanishes to the zero point, as it did in this case, there is only one thing to do: "scrub" the mission. Valuable time was lost while a new operation was mounted. It didn't help General Donovan's temper at all to discover that the eager officer behind this fiasco, a major in our own services, had very thoughtfully provided a monthly item of $500 for himself, over and above his regular army pay and allowances, of course!

And there was the woman who achieved the distinction of being the first American woman captured by the Germans.

A sportswoman of international reputation she had earned her renown honestly. Innumerable big game hunting expeditions into Africa before the war when it was far from the powder-puff operation it is today, had marked her as a woman of courage, resourcefulness and daring. She had joined OSS early, had worked the Washington end and had been sent on to London where she held a position of considerable sensitivity. It wasn't enough. She wanted more action. And as soon as Paris was liberated and an OSS headquarters had been established there, she managed to get herself transferred to the continent.

At that time all civilian personnel in France were required to wear a hybrid uniform as a protective measure. The women had a nondescript WAC outfit without benefit of insignia to be worn at all times. It was fortunate for the episode at hand that our gal was so attired.

On the spur of the moment and certainly without any official knowledge or sanction, she wangled herself a ride in a jeep with two officers who were going on an assignment to the front to the east of Paris. The next we knew was when the word came through that the party had been captured by the Germans. Fortunately for her, because of her uniform, the Germans thought her to be a file clerk and she was smart enough to let them go on believing it.

There was considerable hell to pay back at the Paris office of OSS and even Washington got into the act. Every report, every scrap of news was scanned for any indication as to whether or not the Germans were aware of the fact that they had three persons from OSS in their control, and, it so happened, three persons who could have been valuable prizes had they known. By instinct, not a person at OSS headquarters would discuss the affair or show the slightest recognition of either the incident or the persons involved.

Perhaps the greatest tribute to this woman's courage and daring came from her husband. He was a naval officer then in the Pacific and when he was notified that the Germans had captured his wife his comment was "God help the Germans." His assessment was borne out by events.

Because the Germans were now on the run and certainly because they were unaware of the value of their prize, the confinement was not harsh. Six months after capture our girl friend escaped through Switzerland. How? By getting one of her German captors on her side and then, during a supposed shift of prison locale by train, jumping from the railroad car during a switching interval when the car actually crossed the Swiss border before being re-routed.

Because of the potential danger to any and all OSS personnel being held by the enemy, this young woman was never again permitted to appear at OSS headquarters. She was quickly sent out of Switzerland, back to Paris and then to Washington. German reprisals against any Allied prisoners, once they realized they had been duped, could not be risked by any other course of action.

CHAPTER 7

LA MARCHESA

WE LIKED to think that the Marchesa was for us, the Allied forces, all the way. Certainly, she had helped the Germans, that we knew, and it was for that very reason she was able to be so valuable to OSS.

Perhaps more than anywhere else in World War II, Italy was a ferment of intrigue. From the outset the German-Italian alliance was ill matched: the order-shouting, heel-clicking, stolid and cruel Germans; the easygoing, volatile, life-loving Italians. It was one thing for Hitler and Mussolini to decide to join their countries in war but it was quite a different thing to blend their peoples into a partnership of destruction. It was like trying to make whipped cream stick to rock.

The Marchesa was Italian. The Marchesa hated the Germans, or so she said and her later actions would seem to prove the point. And as an Italian she had that combination of practicality and romance that is the yeast of intrigue. Had it not been for the war, I'm sure the Marchesa would have lived her life through in Italy in the manner of ladies of her class, neither very rich nor very poor. She would have lived on in the city for most of the year; she would have managed a few weeks in the country; she would have entertained a bit in her small circle; she would have been respected in her community and, because of her class, she would be expected to look after those less fortunate in many small ways. As a widow with a family grown and moved away, it would have been a quiet, patterned life. The war changed it, radically.

The Marchesa was in her early sixties when war came. Tall, slender, straight and aristocratic in bearing, she had the fine sharp features and black eyes of a high-born Italian. Although age had taken some of the color from her complexion and left a few small lines instead and although her hair was iron grey and twisted to the top of her head, she had vitality, energy and physical stamina more common in a younger person. And she had an independent spirit and nerve.

"*Si, si,*" she had told us, her eyes penetrating and honest. "I worked with the Germans. But of course . . ." The hands were spread wide in a gesture of frank acknowledgment . . . "that was good for us, no?"

It was good for us. Yes.

When first the Germans came into Italy, more as conquerors than as allies, the Marchesa was quick to sense the snobbery of the officers. A title, such as hers, was an obvious asset, something the rank-conscious Germans instinctively respected. It had shown in her very first contact with them.

In the early days the Germans were of little concern to her. They were there, yes; she saw them in the village near her country place on occasion; and there were more of them to

113

be seen in the city. But contact, either direct or indirect, she did not have—until the day a very scrubbed and polished German officer arrived at her country place and asked to speak with her. He was stiff, correct, almost fawning as he used her title and he wondered if it would be possible to use some of her farm buildings as a temporary, only temporary, billet for a few troops. After all, he informed her, she had a son in the Italian Air Force and she would naturally wish to do everything possible to help the Axis.

So the Germans moved a small communications center into the Marchesa's farm and the quiet of the country was now disturbed by the comings and goings of army vehicles and dispatch riders. The next step could have been guessed without a glimpse of the script. Another stiff, correct but obviously higher ranking German officer arrived to speak with the Marchesa. Her house was large, he observed, much larger than she needed for her own use and certainly too large to maintain with only two elderly servants. It would be most convenient for the German command if they could billet a few officers in the house. The Marchesa, of course, would continue to live in one wing with her servants. The Germans would be meticulous in maintaining their quarters and in observing her privacy. And besides, there would be certain perquisites to her benefit in such an arrangement, ample food supplies, fuel, light, all the things that were becoming more difficult in an Italy at war. The officer was most polite; he made the arrangement sound alluring and he was careful to foster the illusion that the final decision was of course entirely up to the Marchesa. Yet the undertone of the conversation made it perfectly clear that only one decision was possible.

Six German officers moved into her house. It amused her, and infuriated old Maria, her cook, that each officer found it necessary to have his own private room. The Marchesa was now living in a wing to one side consisting of five rooms, an

114

attic loft and two outside entrances. At best it was semi-privacy.

It went on like this for months. The Germans were correct, they were polite, at times almost fawning, but they were in her house and the little irritations occurred. There had been a late, raucous party with prostitutes from the village and the Marchesa complained. Heavy boots, Maria reported, were ruining the parquet floors of the main rooms, and the magnificent panelling was being marred by thumbtacks holding maps, notices and orders. These, the Marchesa told us, she could have forgiven but when the German soldiers billeted in the farm buildings began to taunt Guilio, her farmer, because he was slightly hunched and walked with a limp, then tormented him with crude and cruel practical jokes, she rebelled.

She went directly to the commanding officer billeted in her own house. She was told that he was out for the day. She went again the next day and again she was told he was unavailable. She wrote a note, protesting the treatment of Guilio and asking that the situation be corrected. It went unanswered for four days and then an aide came to tell her that the commandant would see her now. She was ushered into her own drawing room, now an office filled with desks, files and all the confusion of the military and made to feel like a stranger, a suppliant. The officer heard her complaints, assured her with all politeness that something would be done and showed her to the door. As she walked down the hall she could hear his coarse laughter behind her and the mocking accents of her hesitant German. The sadistic ridiculing and tormenting of Guilio went on unchecked.

"La Providenza," the Marchesa said, intervened.

Two nights later Maria tapped lightly on her door and woke her. It was after two o'clock, Maria said, and she hated to disturb la Marchesa but, and she looked furtively about her and spoke softly, Guilio had come to her and said that he had

115

found a wounded parachutist who needed help. He was, Maria added, looking directly at the Marchesa, an American.

The Marchesa sat on the edge of her bed and drew her dressing gown about her. She was a long time in answering Maria while hundreds of conflicting emotions flooded her brain. Danger, hatred, for she now had that for her German "guests," fear, compassion, patriotism, anger, selfishness, self-lessness, they swirled within her while she desperately tried to make a decision. To refuse help would be safe and it could be excused on the basis of patriotism. To give aid would mean danger but it was the way of the heart and it was the way of a mother with a son now flying somewhere at war, perhaps even now in need of just such assistance as was being asked of her.

She told Maria to tell Guilio to bring the wounded man into the kitchen but to be very careful against being observed and above all to make no noise, show no lights. She would help.

La Marchesa had begun her conspiracy to work for the Allies, a course which was to make her a productive OSS agent.

It is a measure of the Marchesa's frankness with us that she confessed that, originally, she had no intention of going any further than offering assistance to this one wounded airman. It was, she insisted, his story, that firmed her in her decision to go on with her role as an Allied agent.

She was in the kitchen with Maria when Guilio brought him in. Without knocking, quickly and silently, the door opened and closed and they were there, Guilio looking worried and yet somehow proudly conspiratorial, the American pale and frightened. He was young, about the age of her Pietro, she guessed. He was dark with short-cropped curly black hair and he was ruggedly built. There was a short growth of beard, a blue-black stubble, and he was dirty. His clothes were ragged and soiled, there was a large, irregular blood stain across his right shoulder and down his arm and he held the arm close to

116

his body in a flexed position. He was obviously suffering much pain.

He smiled and nodded with some embarrassment as the Marchesa came forward and spoke to him in her halting English. To her amazement he replied in good Italian and in a moment the four of them, the Marchesa, Maria, Guilio and the young American were exchanging pleasantries. Maria cooked eggs, made strong coffee, brought milk and cheese and homemade bread and the American ate as if he had never seen food before. It was four days since he had had a meal he told them between gulps of coffee.

When he had finished they inspected his wounds. His shoulder was badly mangled and the ligaments of his arm were shredded. They bathed them with hot water and a solution of home remedies and then bound them with a torn sheet, the two women working silently and deftly, while Guilio watched and the American grimaced against the pain. It was nearly four o'clock when Guilio led him to the loft, gave him a blanket to wrap about him and left.

For three days the Marchesa hid the American, fed him and tended his wounds before she asked him to tell his story. He was stronger now, he had regained his confidence and his wound was certainly no worse, even, they hoped, a trifle better. She asked him, directly, what had happened and what he was doing in the area where no Americans, no Allied troops of any kind had been.

He had parachuted into the country, he confessed, to organize resistance groups, to contact the partisans and to do whatever he could to aid the Allied cause and harass the Germans. He had overshot his drop area, had landed near a German garrison and, in the dark, had been shot at by a sentry. He had run for it and had hidden by day and travelled by night through the rugged mountains without knowing where he was. Exhausted, hungry, weakened from loss of blood, in great pain, he had hidden for a day and a night in a haystack. The haystack happened to be on the Marchesa's property and Guilio had discovered him when he noticed that the stack, which had been untouched for weeks, seemed to have been disturbed at its base.

The American stayed with the Marchesa for another four days and she confessed she enjoyed it. The excitement of the secret, the constant strain of concealment, the serving of clandestine meals and all the rest, appealed to her sense of adventure. It also compensated in some measure for the treatment she had had from the Germans. It gave her a tremendous feeling of power to think that she was playing hostess to enemies.

The young agent was not idle. Maria, who already hated the Germans and everything to do with them, was an easy prey to his influence. She mothered him, protected him, cooked for him and agreed to help in any way. Guilio, after his first tentative contact, finally revealed himself as a full-fledged partisan, until now only casually active. It took little persuading on the part of the American to enlist Guilio's aid. The Marchesa, as she said herself, came into the group, for self-preservation primarily. Obviously, having not turned the agent in when first he appeared at her house, she had forfeited any chance of escaping German wrath and punishment should she now turn him in or be discovered protecting him. But what appealed most, and she said this with a smile, was the thrill she experienced in finding her little incongruous group bound to one another with a fierce, sudden loyalty that all at once had become more important than anything else.

She and Guilio, with their combined knowledge of the area, provided the American with working maps of the rugged countryside around them. They told him where the German and Italian military installations were, what sectors to avoid, where the partisans would be found most cooperative (Guilio was the source here, to the Marchesa's amazement) and dozens of other pertinent facts. They worked out a system of communication by runner with codes and passwords and innumerable

118

other devices to insure the reliability of any cut-outs that might be used. And when everything was ready, the young American took his leave to find his way back to his drop area, recover his hidden gear and begin his mission. He left behind him, with the Marchesa, Guilio and Maria, the core of an espionage and resistance network beyond his wildest dreams.

The Marchesa was now committed and she went to work with gusto. She invited the German commandant to lunch with her in the garden, served by a sullen Maria, but it paid off. The invitation was politely honored with an invitation from the commandant to dine with his staff. An arm-length friendliness developed between the little isolated group of three Italians in the wing and the German officers in the main house. The Marchesa was careful to see that it did not impinge on her privacy and therefore the security of her clandestine operations, but she promoted it to the extent that it gained additional gasoline for her trips into town, for the use of her truck as well as her car and other little amenities.

Now and then the loft provided haven for another visitor, a partisan being hunted, a downed American or British airman, a courier from Giovanni, as the young American who started it all had tagged himself. It amused the Marchesa tremendously to feed these hunted figures from the German larder so amply supplied in the main part of her house. And with each new visitor her excitement mounted, a thrilling sense of participation in something infinitely larger and more important than herself.

By now what had started almost by chance had grown into a full-scale operation of tremendous scope and importance. Two factors, two opposing elements, influenced this growth. Imperceptibly, and yet, in retrospect, unavoidably, the original small German communications center in the farm buildings on the Marchesa's estate had grown until it was now a full-scale operation of real importance to the Axis. At the same time, the increased activity on the part of the partisans and

119

Giovanni, had developed the Marchesa's role into a full-time, highly involved and dangerous operation. That the growth of the communications center hampered the activity of the Marchesa should be obvious. The Germans had surrounded the farm area with a high wire fence and the only gate was now guarded twenty-four hours a day with entry by pass only. The Marchesa, Maria and Guilio were, by courtesy and with exaggerated politeness, allowed to pass freely at any time. So familiar were their figures in their daily comings and goings to and from the village and the lower fields, the guards hardly bothered to look up as they passed. They made the most of this privilege.

The secret visitors still found sanctuary in the loft of the wing. But getting them there became a more delicate and hazardous operation. Fortunately, Guilio lived in a small cottage some distance outside the compound, so his frequent trips through the gate were too numerous to attract notice. It was his idea to use his own deformity as a disguise. And when the first clandestine visitor to arrive after the building of the fence, complete with hunch and limp and with Maria as guide, reached the safety of the Marchesa's kitchen, they were jubilant. It was Maria's triumph when she was able to dress a girl partisan in simulation of herself, ample bosoms and all, so that she could pass unnoticed through the gate with Guilio.

The Marchesa was now running a safe address for OSS agents, a hideout for partisan saboteurs and a stop-over for any Allied airman down in the area. Under the extraordinary circumstances of her establishment, under the noses of a German command, that would seem to be enough. Giovanni had other ideas. He appeared one night with a tiny gadget for the Marchesa to use. Perfected by an OSS expert in electronics, it was a small induction microphone about the size of an ordinary button. A thread-like wire ran from it to an earphone tiny enough to be inserted in the ear and practically invisible. Such was the power of this tiny instrument it could pick up conversation in an adjoining room when placed against the wall or, more important still for what Giovanni had in mind, it could eavesdrop on telephone conversations without having to tap the wires. One only needed to place the microphone within a couple of inches of the phone wire and it would pick up conversation through the insulation! He would see to the installation if the Marchesa would agree to use the gadget and report her findings to a designated letter drop.

Disguised as Guilio, Giovanni spent a busy hour ostensibly cultivating a flower bed not far from the commandant's office, just under the window in fact. And when he had finished his work, mellowing the dirt all the way along the foundations of the house and back to the wing, his installation was complete. He left that evening in time to milk the cows, so that the real Guilio could get on with his work.

It was a tremendous success. With her knowledge of German, the Marchesa was able to listen in on all of the telephone conversations between the communications center and forward operational bases. The flood of information was continuous. Troop movements, personnel shifts, speculation on Allied intentions and possible landings and alternative plans for meeting them, all this the Marchesa overheard and reported.

Then came the exciting day. The landings at Salerno. The Marchesa had had no advance information, of course, but when she heard over the commandant's telephone what was taking place, she felt a sudden exhilaration, a justification for what she had been doing. War was now here, near at hand, with all of the terrible destruction and slaughter magnified a hundredfold because it was at hand and not just something to hear about and comment upon. This, the landing, was to mean the end of the German oppression and, she found herself wishing it, the end of the cancer of fascism in Italy.

It brought war home to her.

The lines from the commandant were now burning with information, reporting on the progress of the landings, calling for reinforcements, organizing the attack that was aimed to push the Allies into the sea. The Marchesa found herself sitting on top of one of the key communications areas figuring in the battle of Salerno. Her own house was the key to the Axis effort against the invasion.

She arranged a meeting in town with Giovanni. It would be dangerous but it was done under the guise of having a minor repair done in her apartment. The workman who came to discuss the repair was Giovanni. He must have been stunned at the nerve displayed by the Marchesa. Her message was brief. It was to tell Giovanni, simply and without argument, that he must get word to the Allied Air Force that the German communications center located in her country house must be destroyed. All that she had overheard pointed to one thing, that this was a key target and key targets, no matter where or what, must be destroyed. Give her two days, just enough time to save a few small, precious belongings and to get Maria and Guilio well away before the bombing started.

Giovanni remonstrated that her value as an agent far outweighed the destruction of the communications center. She answered that she had been long enough at the game now to know relative values. The center must be destroyed.

Two days later Guilio left the farm early and walked into the little village. In midmorning the Marchesa, with Maria beside her in her car, drove through the gate, past the sentry, and down the road. At the village Guilio got in with them and they drove into town.

Late that afternoon a scream of low flying bombers came out of the sun and reduced the Marchesa's country place to rubble.

The Marchesa finished her story. She spooned her gelatti and let the cold linger on her tongue. The tiny sidewalk café was trying desperately to hide the marks of recent war and if you looked off into the distance, across the shimmering blue of the Bay of Naples, it was easy to create the illusion that there had been no war here.

"We admire your heroism. We admire your selflessness. I know I can speak for all Allied forces when I tell you we are grateful for what you have done." General Donovan spoke with that soft modulation of voice which seemed to add emphasis to his words. "I only wish there was some way to recognize your service, some decoration. . . ."

The Marchesa raised her hand and cut him off.

"No, no, no. I want no recognition. For us the war is over. That is enough."

"But after all you have been through." He started to go on but again the hand came up.

"It was better than sitting idle, a lonely widow." She smiled and there was a sly twinkle in her black eyes. "Besides, it was very exciting." She shrugged her shoulders.

The General rose.

"Can we take you somewhere? To your apartment?" He indicated his car standing a short distance away, a sergeant waiting alongside.

"No thank you, General." She held out her hand. "I think I shall just sit here a little while and watch the view. It is so very peaceful. And I am a trifle tired."

General Donovan took her hand in both of his, held it lingeringly and turned to me.

"You stay with the Marchesa, Bob. When she is ready to leave, see her to her apartment. I'll walk back."

The Marchesa watched his erect figure move rapidly down the street.

"The General, he is a wonderful man. He is so good, so kind. It must be very difficult to be a warrior when one is so soft."

She spoke almost to herself, as if I were not there and I made no effort to comment. She was sitting very erect in her chair like the great lady she was. The grey hair, almost white in places, was pulled severely against her head and twisted into a high knot. Her head was high, the nose finely chiseled, the complexion a trifle faded but untouched by artifice. Her black dress was plain and much worn but it had a certain chic.

"I had not the heart to tell him about my Pietro." Her voice was steady but detached. "He was killed in action just a week before it was all over."

CHAPTER 8

THE NEUTRALS

ALTHOUGH it may seem contradictory, in so far as espionage is concerned a neutral country provides greater assistance to a belligerent than its own allies. For, whereas the very act of war has closed all frontiers and raised every conceivable barrier between belligerents, with neutral countries normal relations are continued. Like any really effective intelligence organization, the Office of Strategic Services made the most of the neutral countries. It was a very different type of operation from that directed from a war zone.

It would be relatively safe to say that there were OSS operatives in every sensitive area throughout the world, whether in a belligerent or neutral country. However, our most productive and active neutral bases were in Istanbul, Lisbon, Madrid, Bern and Stockholm. And to any of us regularly assigned to a highly militarized and war-conscious OSS operation such as London, a sudden mission to a neutral country was excitingly different. After all, you knew there would not be a German at the next table to you in a London restaurant, at least not a German-*speaking* one, but after the bombings and the black-outs to sink into the luxury of the Aviz in Lisbon and hear German and Italian being freely spoken around you is, to say the least, unsettling.

Certainly our best known and most productive operation from a neutral country was the mission headed by Allen Dulles at Bern in Switzerland. It was from Bern that agents operating in Germany proper were directed and, because of a common border, it was in Switzerland that we found ourselves in closest touch with the situation in Germany. Dulles built up a network which infiltrated not only Germany but Austria, Hungary, Czechoslovakia, Yugoslavia, Romania, Bulgaria and Greece. Every type of intelligence filtered in from these lines, military, political, economic and sociological, to such an extent that, by the time of the German surrender, OSS was able to supply basic reports for the peace talks which ensued.

It was from the Bern operation that the attempts on Hitler's life were reported and followed with interest. It was Bern that made the first real headway with the German peace feelers in negotiations with Marshall Kesselring, a subject still politically debated. It was Bern that pinpointed for our bombers the rocket launching bases at Peenemunde and the Ploesti oil fields in Romania. And it was from Bern that the greatest supply of Reichsmarks for our agent operations became available.

Istanbul was a vipers nest of intrigue. And perhaps more than in any other outpost one could find every nationality, every shade of political opinion, every type of loyalty, and every type of treachery. It was here, literally, that East met West. Here were not only the German, Italian, American and

126

British agents but the Japs, the Chinese, the Russians, the French, the Scandinavians and the Slavs. It was an international smorgasbord.

Any neutral intelligence post is delicate. Istanbul was maddeningly complex. It is in the nature of a neutral operation to find that, in dealing with one's contacts and "cut-outs" one must of necessity be dealing with persons who are acting in a similar capacity with the enemy. It was part of the value; it was certainly the risk. An OSS operative based in Istanbul, in building an information pipeline, would most certainly know that, even if his own direct contact was a trusted Allied agent, that agent's contact might very well be an enemy double agent. And usually was. These are the situations which offer background for the spy thrillers in the grand manner as borne out by the famous case of "Cicero," the Nazi spy who served as valet to the British ambassador in Istanbul.

A great part of our best intelligence on the Far Eastern situation came out of Istanbul but it was always cross-checked with reports from other networks with greater care than intelligence from almost any other listening post. It was from Istanbul we were able to determine the amount of coordination and cooperation being observed between the Germans and the Japanese. It proved to be less, in actual fact, than the Germans would have wished in their later back-to-the-wall fighting. It was Istanbul that kept an eye on the Middle East for us and reported any and all suspicious movements in that direction. And as still another bank, it was Istanbul that provided the drachma, the dinars, the zlotys and rubles necessary to our work.

Lisbon was an escape hatch to the West and the free world, a trail blazed by the Duke and Duchess of Windsor when first they fled the continent for his assignment as Governor of the Bahamas. This fact, perhaps more than any other, made it an active field for espionage. For while the Allied interests were funneling highly valuable escapee personnel in the nature of atomic scientists, research physicists and the like through Lisbon, the Axis interests were trying to prevent such escapes or at least discover and trace them. It was a cat and mouse game.

Like all of the neutral cities Lisbon was aglitter with the sophistication of an international society but it was a glitter with sinister overtones. Money was the key. Almost anything could be bought in Lisbon from German cameras and Japanese silks to information, assistance and at least temporary allegiance. All of that was important. From the comparison of German products of 1943 and 1944 one could gain valuable information relative to Germany's position in raw materials as indicated by a lessening in quality. Even the workmanship was a giveaway on the manpower position of the Axis. Everything had its story to tell and we had the men to gather the story.

Portugal was the one neutral country from which direct flights to and from the United States were scheduled with any kind of regularity. This fact alone called for an overabundance of Axis observers. And since we, of course, had to have observers to watch the observers, it was a busy and crowded city. No thing, no individual beyond your own immediate range of security-checked personnel could be trusted and the only way to operate in Lisbon, as in fact in any other neutral city, was to assume from the outset that every room was wired for information, that your every move was watched and that, in your absence, every personal item left behind in your quarters was searched. It may not have made for a relaxed way of life but it was the only safe way.

To its own profit, Lisbon played both ends against the middle. One small episode will illustrate the point. An American or Britisher could buy in Lisbon porcelain figurines of Hitler grotesquely hanging from a noose or of Mussolini hysterically haranguing the masses, neither one being flattering in the least. A German or Italian could buy equally unflattering and grotesque figurines of Roosevelt and Churchill. They all made money.

But Lisbon produced vast masses of information for our use from the very beginning. In the early stages of the war it furnished some of the most valuable intelligence relative to the African landings and the subsequent campaign. Information on Vichy France came out of Lisbon as did important data relative to collaborators. It afforded a steady stream of information, some vital, some of background material, on every aspect of the Axis effort. However in one function Lisbon far outperformed other neutral posts and that was in the field of currency supply. For the London operation of OSS from which the bulk of the espionage and sabotage effort on the continent was being mounted, Lisbon supplied the greatest proportion of difficult-to-obtain currencies. It has been pointed out in an earlier chapter how French francs supplied to our agents operating in occupied territory came to us out of Lisbon whence they had been flown by the Germans in their own desperate efforts to obtain much desired currencies to utilize against us.

Madrid, partly because of proximity, worked closely with Lisbon in the development of intelligence networks. Certainly the long common border between Spain and France was a factor in feeding desirable refugee personnel from occupied France into Spain and thence to Lisbon. However, Madrid had an even more vital role to play. Owing to the close collaboration between the German and Spanish Governments during the Spanish civil war, Spain to a much greater degree than perhaps any of the other neutrals was Axis-oriented. It was a situation which suited the needs of an intelligence organization nicely.

From Madrid and from Spanish ports, we were able to obtain information which backed up and amplified our intelligence from Lisbon. Which brings to mind the fact that should be emphasized in the operation of an intelligence organization such as OSS, the need for constant contact and cross-checking between our various listening posts. Although each OSS base operated with a certain amount of autonomy with respect to its own immediate objectives it was in effect only a segment in a larger pattern from which the vital and basic decisions affecting the war effort were to be made. Just as Lisbon and Madrid complemented and back-stopped each other so every intelligence base in the whole vast OSS network complemented and back-stopped every other base to insure the most accurate possible appraisal of the Axis potential.

Madrid kept us informed of the German economic picture. It gave us information to back up the intelligence from Bern on the German political situation. Most important of all, by observing the intensity of German efforts to obtain more and more active support from Spain, it gave us a fairly accurate picture of the increasing desperation within the Nazi war machine.

Because of the importance of Gibraltar the British were especially active in Spain in the intelligence field. It made the coverage pretty complete.

Actually if we could have arranged it to our own satisfaction it is doubtful a more convenient placement of the neutrals could have been worked out. With Istanbul to cover the lower Balkans and the Middle East, Bern on the German doorstep, Madrid to cover southern France and the Western Mediterranean, Lisbon to give us direct access to the Atlantic and our home bases, it only remained for Stockholm to cover the northern perimeter of the war area. This it did, thoroughly.

Stockholm offered a tremendous opportunity for a close observance of the German concentration on the Scandinavian area. It enabled us to obtain a clear picture of German intentions with regard to any attempt to mount an assault from a northern flank in occupied Norway. The intensity of German activity in the obtaining of strategic materials was a clue to the condition of the Nazi war economy. The demand for more foodstuffs, more fuel, more materials of every sort that channelled through Stockholm gave us information which, pieced together with reports from other areas, told the full story.

130

It was from Stockholm that we obtained the overwhelming intelligence relative to the German rocket program which led to the development of the V-1's and V-2's. The fact that we were forewarned, as were the British, considerably offset the potentially devastating effect of these weapons when they were first launched against England. It was from Stockholm that we learned of the German program for the counterfeiting of British currency. It was from Stockholm we were able to liberate key research personnel vital to the development of highly technical war devices.

Strangely, Stockholm seemed least affected by the war around it of any of the neutrals. Whereas Istanbul was obviously seething with intrigue until it almost hung in the air and could be felt on arrival, Stockholm appeared open, friendly, unconcerned with events in a manner inconsistent with the others. Certainly the automobiles were converted to burning wood and all heating, what little was done, was with wood so the effects of war were with them. But there was none of the sidelong glance, whispered, suspicious atmosphere to be sensed in the other cities. They were all there, the German, Italian and Japanese operatives but somehow they seemed less obvious and less sinister but that is not to imply that they were any the less effective, any the less dangerous. One still had to operate under the assumption that every room was wired, every move was watched, everything was searched.

It should be obvious that the type of intelligence obtained through the neutral countries differed considerably from that obtained in enemy territory. What the neutrals could offer was the general trend in affairs within the enemy camp. In its dealings in neutral markets, in financial transactions, in diplomatic and political maneuvering, the Axis revealed to us general factors which, when coupled with specifics gathered from other sources, amounted to knowledge. It was unlike the intelligence sent back from our agents operating within Germany and

131

the occupied countries where the information was direct and specific. But either one without the other was weakened.

Similarly, the agent operating in a neutral country followed a rather different procedure. In many instances he quite openly made contacts which could in turn lead to other and hidden sources of information. Certainly his nationality was no secret nor was it disguised as was universally the case of an agent on mission in enemy territory. It gave him more flexibility but it demanded as much in the way of discretion and caution. His intelligence tended more to political, economic and social factors whereas the agent operating in enemy country was primarily interested in intelligence of a military and strategic importance.

Perhaps the most important single factor marking the difference between a neutral and a belligerent operation lay in the support and supply of resistance groups. Obviously, in the neutral country, there was no operation of this kind which immediately reduced the size of the mission and the military flavor which characterized those OSS bases aimed in enemy territory. Had support of military action taken place directly from any of the neutral countries not only would the neutrality of the country be endangered but the operation itself would have been outlawed by the neutral. Neither would have been to our advantage and at all times OSS operatives were careful to observe and preserve the neutrality of the country from which they functioned.

There was one ready-made network of potential espionage agents waiting to be organized for the Allied war effort throughout Europe. With members and representatives numbering in the thousands, they existed in every country from Norway to Greece. In occupied countries, in neutral countries, in Germany and Italy as well, organized "cells" were there needing only direction. OSS decided to supply that direction.

This huge, sprawling network was the International Transport Workers Federation. As an international labor union, this organization held as members any workers in the various fields of transport. Railroads, trucking, inland barges, sea-going ships and planes, all the elements of transportation came under the wing of this union. And within each special field every type of worker from the baggage heaver through engineers, clerks, wireless operators and dispatchers were included. Not only did they have knowledge of all the transport systems throughout Europe, they had free access to all the facilities. It offered a heady opportunity.

General Donovan moved in fast on it. Early in 1942 the plan was worked out and within a matter of weeks it was operational. From London, on a regional basis, use was made of innumerable enthusiastic volunteers provided from the ranks of this union. It flourished and burgeoned until it seemed as if there was not a segment of the European transport map that we did not cover or could not reach.

Through these operatives we were constantly and almost immediately aware of some of the most important factors in the Nazi war effort. Principal supply depots were pinpointed. Traffic, to and from these points, indicating build up or withdrawal, was reported on. The direction of mass shipments of any strategic material was reported and indicated the military intentions of the enemy. Hidden plants manufacturing secret components were pinpointed for our bombers with special attention to synthetic rubbers, oils and steel. And through sea cargoes and ship loadings the whole vast picture spread around the world, just who dealt with the Axis in what categories and to what extent. It made some of the targets almost too easy for our planes.

Over and above the work within the framework of the union, innumerable recruits were trained and dropped with our espionage and sabotage teams as an aid to the destruction of the more important communications centers on the continent, both within Germany and the occupied countries.

There were those who charged that the union was a communist-dominated organization. There were undoubtedly many communists within its fold. But it offered, as did no other element in Europe, men ready and willing to act against the Axis. They had the vast added advantage of being on the spot, at the enemy's jugular vein.

General Donovan gave the critics short answers. To the charge that OSS was funding communist groups, his reply was quick and to the point.

"I'd put Stalin on the OSS payroll," he said, "if I thought it would help us defeat Hitler."

CHAPTER 9

CHETNIKS AND PARTISANS

IN THE WILD, wet, plunging blackness of the night sea, it seemed almost impossible to discover the coast-line, certainly impossible to make a landing. No lights. No lights anywhere, no running lights on the small craft, no distant lights ashore, no stars, nothing but blackness, wet and howling.

The Adriatic. The Dalmatian Coast. Romantic sounding names they had always been, it seemed, as long as they were unknown. But now, real and forbidding and challenging, known but not understood or familiar, they were hateful, fearful, dread places. Until you found one of those hidden, protected coves and then all of a sudden it became romantic again and you were ready to do it all over.

135

At least that's what Steve thought.

He stood beside the weathered, wrinkled, leather-faced Yugoslav at the tiller of the small craft and peered ahead into the black. He gripped the bar before him to steady himself against the pitch and whip of the boat and despite his foul weather gear he could feel the wet trickle down his neck. He wasn't sure whether it was rain or spray or both and it didn't really matter, it was wet and it was cold and it was a damned dismal, uncomfortable business.

It was always like this. One hundred and fifty miles, give or take a few, that was the run from southern Italy across the Adriatic Sea to the Dalmatian coast. It seemed like one hundred and fifty years in time, years engulfed in black, wet discomfort when, for hours on end, one seemed suspended in a huge void without direction. Just a huge void that surged up and down with a sickening side-slip plunging into nowhere. A kind of wet treadmill, that's what it was, he thought.

It seemed incredible that one could go on peering into a black nothingness until the eyes ached, probing for a known object and then be surprised when it appeared. But it always did surprise him, try as he might to be ready for it.

There it was again, all of a sudden. Blacker than the night, hanging over the little fishing boat like a threat of cloud were the forbidding mountains, the Montenegro mountains, so aptly named. Three, four thousand feet, more, they seemed to slide out of the clouds directly into the sea. By day they would be forbidding grey with rock, bleak, almost devoid of any green except for serried terraces of vineyards. But now they were huge black masses without any distinguishable features beyond the irregular rounded outline of their summits against the dark but now slightly paler sky.

They were running in close now for Steve could see the sudden white flame of spray against rock as the sea broke against the foot of the cliffs. The Yugoslav skipper reduced his speed and let his craft settle into the surf while he searched the gloom for the landmarks he knew would guide him in. They were running parallel to the shore line, bucking the heavy sea and catching great whiplashes of spray while the wind gusted about them, down-drafted from the cliffs above and wailed out to sea only to return laden with water.

Like a blind man feeling his way along a wall to a door, the skipper eased his boat down the shore line. Then he found it. A quick change of direction and they eased through a narrow channel between two towering shafts of rock into a small cove. It was like another world. No wind. No heavy sea. No wild, wet, screaming, plunging progress that seemed to be no progress. On all sides, like the walls of some huge fortress, the rock cliffs rose straight from the sea. It was, Steve always thought, like being at the bottom of one's own enormous private well with a secret exit to the world beyond.

Everything was suddenly tranquil. The skipper cut his engines and let the little craft drift. The soft sizzling of the hull slithering through the water, the occasional slap of a vagrant wave against the boat, the subdued voices of the men, only this after the hours of buffeting, howling open sea.

Black, black, black. So black and still, the dark, starless sky almost seemed bright against the hovering bulk of the cliffs. Then, for an instant only, a tiny pinpoint of light speared the darkness and was gone. It was off a bit to the left, on the shore line. In the vast cavern of the hidden harbor it seemed no more than the fleeting flicker of a firefly. It came again, two short stabs of light this time and then darkness again, more intense than ever.

Steve watched it and waited. One, one two. In quick succession the light blinked again, waited and then blinked once more, a single shaft.

Steve took his flashlight and answered. Two short bursts of light, a pause, two short bursts again. Darkness.

From shore came an answering steady beam, sweeping the water in an arc, lingering over the black glass surface and then out.

The skipper started his engine. It seemed to reverberate in the cavern of the deep harbor and he tried to silence the exhaust by just barely sliding over the water. Steve motioned him on. They were in, they had been coded, they had replied and they were clear. There was no use in delaying the job now. This was the payoff. It was also the moment that Steve enjoyed, the moment when all the romance that he had always associated with the Adriatic Sea and the Dalmation Coast came flooding in on him. Not the romance of the travel posters. Not the romance of far-off places. This was his own special brand of romance, a kind only a limited few would ever know, had ever seen.

He watched for it now, knowing how it would all begin, how it would be played out, much as one anticipates an oft-seen and well-loved play. He waited and listened, straining to see and to hear while the boat made its slow, steady, quiet way in to shore. Then, almost dead ahead and right on the shore line the first flare flamed into yellow brilliance. Another flared beside it. Then two more, a boat's length from the first two, flamed and sent off trailing, curling pennants of heavy black smoke. He could see figures now moving back and forth on the little jetty on the shore and he could hear the shouts, too far off to be intelligible but clear enough to convey the excitement in the tone.

Then, as if an unseen hand were lighting some giant birthday cake, the flares came alight. Starting from the shore as if someone were running along a line and igniting them, the flaming yellow torches climbed and snaked up the mountainside, doubling back, disappearing, showing again higher up and smaller now, until a thin ribbon of flickering light wreathed the bold rock face of the mountain like a garland.

138

And all the while the mirror of the quiet water in the harbor repeated the pattern at his feet until the whole area flickered and glowed with the gay unreality of a dream world.

Steve stood, as he always did, fascinated and thrilled by the scene. And as always, he wondered at the incongruity of it all, this queer alliance of patterned pageantry and secret war. Here he was, bringing in a boatload of arms and ammunition for the Yugoslav partisans, secretly supplying resistance to the Germans and it was being received with all the excitement and celebration of a carnival.

They were in close now and the skipper was bringing the boat alongside the jetty. It was a makeshift affair of broken stones and gravel jutting out into the harbor just far enough for the boat to come in safely without danger of scraping bottom. A small, wild, unused and uninhabited cove, the Yugoslavs had chosen it because it was inaccessible and remote, completely unheeding of the tremendous physical effort involved in getting the supplies up out of the area and distributed to the resistance groups. The flares? Safe enough. No one comes anywhere near this area, certainly no Germans, they had assured us.

With all of the skill and confidence of hardened fishermen, they brought the boat to a mooring. Lines were snugged. Gangplanks were laid down. Commands were spoken, not shouted. The unloading began.

The system had been worked out for the very first supply mission and it was a miracle of efficiency. Starting at the very edge of the dock a line of strong, rugged and unspeaking men lined the torch-lighted path that wound up the mountainside. In the manner of the old-fashioned bucket brigade the heavy pieces, the heavy guns, the ammunition boxes, the explosives, were handed from one to another up the winding, tortuous face of the looming mountain. Once started, the whole operation took on a rhythm that could be readily seen as it heaved,

139

swung and hoisted each piece from one man to another, rising, rising, and twisting in the soft yellow glare of the torches.

At the same time another operation was in progress. Young boys, girls, women, all sizes, shapes and ages, filed past the little ship. Each one hoisted some piece of equipment from the deck of the boat, turned and started back up the path. In this way the smaller, lighter supplies were unloaded and transported to the top of the mountain to be distributed to the group leaders and to be cached until used.

Within a half hour the cargo of war supplies had been unloaded and the small ship was riding high in the water, ready for its return to base. On the jetty one of the leaders broke open a small cask of strong red wine and offered drinks to Steve, to his Yugoslav skipper and to his helpers. They smiled at each other, nodding their heads and making sign language for Steve. They were sweating, their bare shoulders were glistening in the glare of the torches and they wiped at their foreheads with their forearms.

They shook hands all round with exaggerated smiles to bridge the language gap. The lines were cast off, the engines caught and they were under way, slowly, serenely. The shore line receded rapidly as they swung out into the harbor and headed for the narrow channel that would take them into the open sea. Up the face of the mountain, in the glow of the flares, Steve could see the spasmodic motion of colored scarves and kerchiefs as the partisans waved them off. And on the little jetty the small group of leaders, waving and watching them disappear into the black of the harbor night. The line of flickering, twisting flares curled up the mountain and danced in the wake of the boat.

Then, one by one, they started to go out. First the four torches on the jetty. They flamed bright for an instant and were gone. Next the torches on the path at the base of the mountain flared and died. And while he watched, Steve could see the trailing filament of light grow gradually shorter and shorter like a burning string until the last one at the summit flared and went out.

Darkness spilled over everything. After the brilliance of the flares the mountains were no longer visible; there seemed to be no way to distinguish the harbor from the mountains and the sky. They were once again groping their way in blackness and the pageantry of moments before, the romance of the setting, the urgency of the mission, the intensity of the Yugoslavs had vanished.

Ahead lay the open sea, rough, dark, wet and forbidding.

OSS was operating agents in North Africa in 1942. By early spring of 1943 the organization was functioning productively as an espionage and sabotage agency throughout northern Europe. By late spring of 1943 we had effective missions in Sicily and Italy. With the landings at Salerno in early September of 1943 and the separate surrender of Italy in that same month, OSS, by a leapfrog action, got under way in an effort to infiltrate the Balkans.

The spearhead was an OSS base at Bari on the Adriatic Coast just above the heel of the Italian boot. As General Donovan was quick to point out, it was about one hundred and fifty miles across the Adriatic Sea from southern Italy to the Dalmatian Coast of Yugoslavia. It would be "relatively simple," in the words of General Donovan, to get agents onto Yugoslav soil either by direct landings across the sea or by drops.

Although deserted by the Italians, the Germans were fighting every inch of the way back up the length of Italy. In the best tradition of OSS aims and purposes it was obvious that the organizing of resistance groups within Yugoslavia would considerably aid the Allied cause by harassment of the Germans in another vital area. In short, what we had been doing throughout Italy and France, in fact wherever Germans were on alien soil, could now be done effectively in Yugoslavia.

Certainly the Yugoslavs should have furnished fertile territory for the organization of resistance groups, of sabotage against the Germans and the like. Germany had been ruthless in its conquest of the country in the spring of 1941. The Yugoslav capital, Belgrade, had been demolished to rubble in a matter of hours under the assault of Hermann Goering's Luftwaffe and the people of Yugoslavia, tough, independent and resourceful, had felt the repressive measures of Hitler's bully boys and sadists for a long two years.

Our intelligence reports out of Yugoslavia were telling us that the country was ripe for the organization of resistance groups, that all they needed were leaders, arms and munitions and basic instruction in the use of our equipment. The Yugoslav spirit and hatred of the German invaders would do the rest. OSS began to supply the sabotage instructors and, more important, the small arms, the munitions and the explosives.

We had failed to reckon with the internal political intrigues of opposing factions within the country. To our bitter surprise we learned that there were partisans and partisans, that there were groups within groups waging all-out battle for control of the country. What the Germans had denied them, arms and the means to enforce their rule, we had supplied in good faith in the hope and on the supposition that it would be used against the common enemy, Germany. The treachery that was Yugoslavia did otherwise.

The first OSS contact with the partisan groups in Yugoslavia had been tentative. The units were isolated; to a great extent they were without any real organization and they were ill-equipped. But they had a fighting spirit. In a sense many of them were in the nature of brigand bands, tough, independent fighters unwilling to submit to any authority. However they had been organized partially under the domination of a native leader of vigor and drive, General Draza Mihailovic.

The young King Peter had fled his country at the time of

the German occupation, first seeking asylum in Egypt and later spending the duration of the war in London. Mihailovic was King Peter's Minister of War in the Yugoslav Government-in-exile. In this position, left behind in the country, he had moved to organize a resistance to the Germans through the Chetniks, as his followers were called.

Our supplies were fed in to him and his Chetnik bands. Night after night, small craft had put into the hidden harbor on the Montenegran coast and Steve and his co-workers unloaded the weapons, steel and explosives necessary for a tough resistance campaign against the Germans. All of the vast complex of OSS sabotage instruction and organization began to function in this newly opened area for the harassment of the enemy.

But Mihailovic had tough and ruthless opposition among his own people within the country. That opposition was led by Tito, a Yugoslav-born, Soviet-trained Communist. The basic raison d'être within each group was of course the decimation and defeat of the German forces occupying the country. But then, at first imperceptibly, and then with a stronger current, other factors began to influence the action and direction of these opposing resistance groups. Those factors were determined by the ruthless internal struggle between Mihailovic and Tito for power and the final total control of Yugoslavia.

Considerably prior to OSS activity, the British services operating within the country were supplying assistance to both Mihailovic and Tito in the natural assumption that they would work together for the defeat of the common enemy. OSS contact had been made only with Mihailovic. It was to his group that our supply missions and sabotage organizers were being sent.

Then, as the sinews of resistance grew and more supplies came into the hands of more people, a strange undercurrent developed. We discovered that our material was being sold

143

to opposing partisan groups under Tito. At first it seemed a sporadic type of treachery. But then, as the tension grew, it became obvious that Yugoslavs were beginning to fight Yugoslavs. And with weapons supplied on the one hand by OSS and on the other to a great extent by the British services. A full-scale civil war was in the offing.

Our intelligence was informing us of the treachery of both sides. Mihailovic was submitting to a ruthless type of German blackmail involving the lives of friends and relatives in exchange for collaboration. Tito was fighting Mihailovic with weapons which his partisans had stolen or bought from his (Mihailovic's) men, weapons which OSS was supplying in the most hazardous manner.

General Donovan was infuriated by the treachery. OSS was risking the lives of dozens of young Americans and innumerable other patriots, Italian, Yugoslav, French, in an effort to drive the Germans out of Yugoslavia. He was not in any way interested in building up one potential Yugoslav leader against the other in a game of power politics. Certainly he was not going to give an assist to a civil war. And he was repelled by the idea that his men were risking their lives in order that unscrupulous individuals within Yugoslavia could make a profit.

Fortunately, the situation had reached such proportions that it had to be resolved at the highest command levels. Through the influence of none other than Prime Minister Churchill the British support of Mihailovic was withdrawn and the nod was given to Tito. The pressures put upon the indecisive and immature King Peter to dismiss his Minister of War, Mihailovic, are well-known. It took months of talk and persuasion to accomplish that end but in the meantime the real problem of the internal resistance to the Germans in Yugoslavia was solved.

OSS abruptly withdrew from the scene. Our contact had been with Mihailovic. The Allies, led by the British, had decided to back Tito. It was felt that the effectiveness of our operation would now be limited insofar as there would certainly be a coolness and mistrust of OSS operatives on the part of Tito. The organization of sabotage, the supply of resistance forces, all of the complex and clandestine support of the Yugoslav effort was henceforth in the hands of the British services.

Back in London the young King Peter was living in luxurious exile at Claridges. He wanted very much to have a flying suit exactly like those issued to the American pilots. After much high-level wangling a suit was produced and he immediately put it on and strutted about his suite like a small boy with his first cowboy suit.

It seemed to make little difference that the suit was much too large for his slender, undersized frame.

As far as my own work was concerned, I now found myself involved, at General Donovan's direction, with the Yugoslav court-in-exile. It was perhaps the most pleasant assignment of the war for me.

The small group consisted of King Peter, a slight, rather nervous, indecisive young man; his Queen, Alexandra, a tall, slender, svelte brunette with expressive eyes; and her mother, the Princess Aspasia of Greece, a handsome, dark-haired woman of elegant figure and bearing. The Princess Aspasia was the dominant element. A woman of intelligence, she was decisive, shrewd and courageous. Her daughter, the young Queen, had much of her character but without the maturity. Between them they were a strong force to bolster the King.

Over the months we had many meetings, but certainly the most amusing was a small *diner à quatre* in their suite at Claridges. I couldn't help but wonder what one did with royalty after dinner. After all, there were only the four of us and, though the conversation had been bright during dinner, it seemed only logical that we might end up at bridge.

145

The Princess Aspasia took command.

As the coffee was being served in the drawing room, she turned to me with a smile.

"Bob," she asked, in her soft voice with the attractive accent, "Have you ever seen the Yugoslav crown jewels?"

My first reaction was to pose in my mind the question as to just where I, from the Connecticut countryside, would have ever encountered the Yugoslav crown jewels. I replied that I didn't believe I had ever had that pleasure.

"Peter, get them," she said with a graceful wave of a hand.

The young king left the room and returned shortly toting a large, obviously heavy, locked casket. He placed it on the floor before the Princess Aspasia, dropped to one knee, fumbled with a bunch of keys from his pocket and opened the lid.

It was quite a sight. There were jewels of every size and description. Diamonds, emeralds, sapphires, rubies, they were in tiaras, necklaces, earrings, bracelets and brooches. There were matching sets to be worn on state occasions and there were individual items of great importance.

The young Queen, Alexandra, bent over the casket gleefully telling over the contents. At random she withdrew an enormous, glittering necklace of huge sapphires surrounded by diamonds, the stones growing larger and larger as they descended to a sort of pendant at the center. It was the kind of bauble one would have called in the gay nineties a stomacher.

Alexandra held it to her throat, her hands at the back of her neck, her elbows out. With her head held high, her eyes flashing, her whole face vibrantly alive, she walked quickly back and forth across the room, her lithe, slender figure graceful in every motion.

She paused for a moment before a large glass, then turned back to us and stepped before the Princess Aspasia.

"Mama, how do I look?"

146

The Princess Aspasia drew herself up on the divan, her black eyes snapping, her elegantly coiffed head shaking forcefully.

"No, no, no, no, darling." Her voice was firm and she placed her coffee cup on the table before her. Then, rapidly tapping her bosom with both hands in a kind of fluttering motion, she went on, "You are not beeg enough here."

CHAPTER 10

ADRIENNE

WE FOUND her in the horror hell of Dachau.

As the Allied Armies advanced in the final days of the war the collapse of the Nazi forces brought panic to the bully-boy staffs of the concentration camps. Here the rotten sadism of the Nazi regime reached its nadir. Buchenwald, Belsen, Auschwitz and Dachau and countless other torture camps would reveal to all the world the depraved cruelty of the Nazi "super-race." Aware of their monstrous guilt, the commandants made one final effort to wipe out all witness to their revolting crimes. The gas chambers worked to capacity around the clock and still they were unable to consume them all, the unfortunate prisoners of the master race.

148

I shall never forget General Donovan's arrival at Dachau. Word had come through that Adrienne had been found alive and, impulsively, General Donovan decided that he would go to see her. He had a special interest in Adrienne. She had been dropped into Belgium months before and had vanished completely without once making contact with London. We had quite naturally assumed that she had been killed in her drop although we never felt really comfortable with that decision because her two team-mates had vanished as silently and completely as she.

The German countryside beyond Munich seemed serene and untouched as we sped along the road toward Dachau and it was difficult to believe that the most dreadful war of all time had been fought in this land. Trees were in heavy foliage, fields lay rich under the mellow sun and even the stark barracks of Dachau, behind their high barriers of barbed wire, looked ordinary rather than sinister as we approached.

The sight that met our eyes moments later was all the more shocking as a result. Army personnel, mounted on huge bull-dozers, were pushing high stacks of rotting bodies into enormous pits which had been scooped out of the soft earth. Most of the men were wearing gas masks against the stench and the rest had covered their faces and nostrils with handkerchiefs.

General Donovan stared in horrified silence for a moment and then turned to me.

"Dear God, Bob. Can you believe this? And it's only one camp out of many."

He pulled out his handkerchief and held it to his nose. I followed suit and we both turned away from the hideous sight.

An orderly took us to a barracks at some distance from the bulldozing operation where a temporary army hospital had been fitted up. Already some of the more fetid of the prisoners barracks, where they had been housed on plank bunks six deep along the walls, were in flames. And in the distance, knowing

149

instinctively what they stood for, we saw the high stacks looming above the low buildings which housed the gas chambers.

I had seen Adrienne once in London with General Donovan. She was tall and slender with an attractive figure. Her hair was dark and worn in a long bob, softly curling, and she had pale blue eyes, the envy, I'm sure, of every brunette who ever knew her. She was not beautiful, nor really pretty, but she had clear, highly colored skin, good teeth in a quick smile, and a vivacity which made her seem prettier than she was. At twenty-eight she had background, education and high intelligence. This was the picture I carried in my mind as we went into the hospital.

It was not what General Donovan and I saw when the orderly finally stopped by a bed at the end of a long room.

On the pillow before us lay a head with no hair on it whatsoever. The pale blue eyes were staring wildly from deeply sunken sockets that seemed to be ringed with black kid. The cheeks were grey and sunken and there were no teeth in the face at all so that the once full mouth had fallen in on the gums in the grotesque manner of advanced age.

If General Donovan was as shocked as I, he well concealed it. He had slipped off his service cap, tucked it under the belt of his tunic and stepped toward the bed.

"Adrienne." His voice was firm but soft. "Adrienne, Minette." I could almost feel the warm paternal surge within him.

The tiny, grotesque, wasted head turned toward him, the staring eyes rolled into focus and there was a sudden gasp and a sudden reaching of skeletal hands.

"Mon General. Mon General Donovan. You are here. And I am alive."

General Donovan took her hand and sat on the edge of the bed beside her. Slowly, quietly and firmly, he talked to her with the wonderful mellowness of his voice. He told her that she would soon be taken back to a real hospital where she could rest and gain her strength. He told her, and I crossed

150

my fingers for him, that she looked fine and would soon be well again.

She clung to his hand as he rose from the bed and implored him with her eyes not to leave. He held her hand for a few lingering moments while he explained to her that the war was all but over, that he must leave now so that she could rest and then, in a short while, when she was well, he would see her again.

And so we left.

Back past the still laboring bulldozers at their grisly task, past the stench and the horror, past the barbed wire barricades and finally out onto the open road. We rode back to our plane in unbroken silence.

There was nothing to be said.

It was many weeks before Adrienne was strong enough to tell her story. She had been brought back from Dachau and given the ultimate in care. General Donovan saw that she was fitted with a full set of teeth, a full wig to conceal her cropped hair and fresh, feminine clothing. As soon as she had been medically cared for she was taken from the institutional environment of a hospital and lodged in one of the OSS rest areas maintained in England for agent personnel. Here she was allowed complete freedom to rest, read, work in the garden, take walks, listen to music, do anything she wished to bring her back to normalcy and to erase the horrors of the Nazi torture camps. Then, as her strength increased and she began to gain weight, there were trips up to London for the theater and what other diversion she wished. But no reference, on Donovan's insistence, should be made to her mission. For us the days dragged on.

Adrienne had been one of a team of three. But she was the key. I remember General Donovan telling me that her father, a Belgian businessman, had been a personal friend of many years. Donovan had known Adrienne, Minette as her family called her, from childhood, had watched her grow and develop with great pride. Then, when suddenly she appeared in war-time London and volunteered for an assignment with OSS, he had refused to consider her offer. It was too much like sending his own daughter on a hazardous mission.

But Adrienne persisted. She had been caught in London at the outbreak of the war, had stayed on and then, with the collapse of France and the low countries, found it impossible to return to her native Belgium. She spoke fluent English, French, German and Italian. She was matured, well-educated and talented and her intelligence was considerably above average. Coupled with her personal charm and vitality, she possessed the disciplined body of a natural athlete. All this, added to the courage which her insistence implied, made a most tempting agent package. General Donovan decided to form a mission around her.

Many of our most successful operations had been team assignments, the use of three persons dropped together, one to handle espionage, one to do sabotage and one to act as radio contact with London base. Such teams worked and trained as a group and yet, for security reasons and for their own safety in the field, no member of the team knew more than the barest outline of the other members' real objectives. Thus, the espionage agent knew only his own assignment and was unaware of his sabotage-teammate's job. Just so, the radio code man was a service operative unaware of the full objectives of his two teammates. It was decided that Adrienne should go in with two teammates, she to be the espionage agent, one to be a sabotage agent and the third to be radio contact.

Pierre was chosen for the sabotage assignment. He was a husky, attractive young Belgian recruited in London and sent through our sabotage training schools. He learned everything —the uses of explosives, the value of emery dust or even ordinary sand in delicate machinery, water or a lump of sugar (if such a prize should be obtainable in a war-rationed economy) in a gasoline tank, how to kill silently and unexpectedly, in short all the devious terrifying methods of hit and run destruction. Obviously, none of this had been taught him until his background, motives and general security had been thoroughly checked and re-checked.

He was a good student, Pierre, and he had dash. There was a certain bravado in the way he carried out some of his training assignments and he had to be cautioned against his tendency to flamboyance. But he had nerve, a cool head and a body developed and coordinated to perfection. He was bilingual in French and German, a definite advantage in his mission, so the fact that his English was faulty was of no concern.

Georges was picked for the radio man. And he was a natural. At thirty-two, he had several years behind him as a radio technician and repairman in his native Belgium. Unlike Adrienne and Pierre, Georges was married with a wife and child somewhere in occupied Europe, he knew not where. His own story of his escape from the Germans was told in quiet understatement which belied the dangers he had faced.

He was tall, lithe and notably handsome. He had a straight, very fine nose with sharply cut nostrils which he dilated sensitively as he spoke. His eyes were almost the pale tawny color of his light brown hair which was thinning a trifle, straight and carefully groomed. Georges, one seemed to sense, was vain and he was perhaps overly attentive to the delicacy of his hands with their long, slender, artistic fingers. But then, he prided himself on his "touch" with a sending key, so it was only natural that he should be aware of their value.

Georges' training was the easiest of the three. After all, it was not necessary to teach him how to repair or reconstruct a radio, that he already knew as he knew almost everything there was to know about radio. But he did have to learn our special code, worked out for his particular mission and designed to defy any attempt to break it. Only through his mas-

153

tery of the code could the intelligence garnered by Adrienne be transmitted back to London. Only through his code could Pierre ask for future "drops" of supplies for his sabotage. But Georges was an alert student and he learned his codes well and swiftly.

The team was ready to put together. Up to this point the three members had been training separately in the specifics of their assignments. To be sure they already knew each other under their "cover" names and histories, they were living in the same area and they were having their meals and free time together. But now, the last days before they were to be dropped, they were spending all day together on their general over-all mission.

It was an attractive team. Both men naturally took to Adrienne. Each one privately had been cautioned by his briefing officer against emotional involvement and she had the good sense to play the sister act, teasing, laughing and bantering with them in an open and carefree manner that precluded serious attachment.

This is the point where the real life espionage operation takes leave of the fictional one. Always in the great spy stories there is the love angle, the involvement of spy with spy or agent with quarry. That is for the devotees of cloak-and-dagger fiction. In real life, in the sophisticated, productive and successful operation of a male-female espionage team the agents concerned are intelligent enough to realize that their very survival depends on controlling their emotions. Adrienne, Pierre and Georges were those intelligent agents.

They built among themselves a strong bond of loyalty, companionship and devotion. But it was not endangered by any love angle. Not that the ingredients were not there. They were. And in force. Adrienne was a delightful, amusing and intelligent young woman, without beauty but with real charm and warmth. Both Pierre and Georges were full-blooded men. Pierre, attractive in a boyish way but not handsome, filled with vitality and enthusiasm, Georges, handsome almost to the point of elegance, quiet, assured. Either man would arouse the interest of any normal young woman and surely Adrienne had enough and more to stimulate the average male. It was a credit to their superior intelligence that each one, quietly and without stated purpose, kept full emotional control.

Adrienne's target area was to be near Maastricht, close to the Belgian-German border and not too far from Aachen. The area was familiar to her and supposedly, with her facility with German, it would be possible for her to work her way into Germany proper. Her schooling in espionage had indicated how best she might work her way into some position from which she could observe and report enemy military movement and potential but its exact implementation would be up to her. With previous clerical and secretarial experience it was hoped that she might be able to find herself employment to our advantage.

Pierre would operate within the same general area but independently of Adrienne. It would be up to him to probe the possibility of organizing and developing resistance workers and to sabotage wherever and whatever would be most telling in its effect.

Georges would maintain contact with both Adrienne and Pierre, separately, with the emphasis being on the importance of their not being openly associated. So, they were briefed and readied.

Again it was the dark of the moon. To the pilots of the big bombers fitted with the "joe hole," the drop flights had become so numerous and so routine as to be almost boring in their pattern. But for each agent and each team sent out there was nothing routine and certainly nothing boring in the start of a mission into enemy territory. Everything now was ready. There was the nervously bright dinner at the holding area where the tension was always just under surface, held from breaking out by the individual courage and effort of each person present. Then came the dressing of the agents, the final checking of all gear and equipment, the donning of the camouflage smocks, the crash helmets and the parachutes.

Things were moving swiftly and with precision now. The huge bomber rumbled into position before the flight shack, there were the quick, firm and yet almost diffident handshakes, the murmured good wishes, the climb up the ramp and into the plane without another glance to the rear.

And then, so suddenly it hardly seemed to have had time to reach the end of the runway, there was the crashing roar of take-off.

Adrienne, Pierre and Georges were airborne.

The drop had been routine. That much we knew. The pilot and crew of the bomber reported that everything had gone with precision. The night had been dark but clear all the way, they came in almost directly on target, quickly lined up the pinpoints of signal light flashed by the ground agents and made their glide. Adrienne was the first to jump and she was followed by Georges and then Pierre.

As far as London was concerned they had jumped into oblivion. The early delay in contact was not disturbing. Any number of factors could have explained a failure of immediate radio contact, broken transmitter during the drop, suspicion which demanded hiding out for a few days, perhaps an injury which was taking attention, every possible explanation was examined. But the hours became days, the days became weeks, and there was no word. Adrienne, Pierre and Georges had vanished and they were given up as one of those things we always knew could happen but always hoped wouldn't.

It was not to be wondered that General Donovan was anxious to get the full story from Adrienne. It was not a pretty one.

As the pilot had reported, Adrienne had been the first to jump and she was followed, as we had been told, by Georges

156

and then Pierre. Her drop was easy. She had not been dragged and she had quickly taken off her harness and 'chute, her jump slacks, her camouflage smock and helmet and buried them. After the tension of the flight it had felt good to be physically active again and she dug with a certain satisfaction. She felt so well she had to restrain herself from humming as she worked. How long? Ten minutes, perhaps fifteen. It was such a lovely night, it was all so quiet after the roar of the plane and it all seemed so natural and logical to be digging in a field in Belgium. Time really mattered very little.

When she had buried the tell-tale parachute she remained for a moment on her knees and peered around her into the darkness. This, she knew, could be the most dangerous time of all for an agent, but it gave her confidence to know that some-where nearby, in the same field and burying their own gear, were Pierre and Georges. Soon they would make brief contact, find their bearings and arrange for a future rendezvous. She stretched out flat on the field and gazed up at the stars. The night now seemed almost too bright for a "drop" and yet they had made it. Successfully.

The thought made her stir uneasily. Quite suddenly, the almost complete stillness of the night became disturbing and ominous. Where were Pierre and Georges? Where were the ground agents who had pinpointed the drop area for them? Why was everything so oppressively silent?

Anxiously, she rose on one elbow and squinted into the darkness across the field against the horizon. No sound. No motion. Then, suddenly, just to her left, she heard the soft sound of someone walking across the field. The steps were slow and tentative and she waited, holding her breath. Nearer now, the figure came, almost toward her and yet, she was sure, if she stayed motionless, his course would carry him past her without her being observed. She tried to hold her breath but her heart was pounding so strongly in her temples she could hardly catch another sound. The figure came closer, half crouching, peering into the darkness. Yes, it was! No. Yes!

"Pierre."

She slivered the word through her lips, hoping it would and wouldn't be heard, afraid that perhaps it wasn't Pierre after all.

The figure dropped to the ground, silently, and there seemed to be hours and hours of agonizing silence while she watched and waited and while he scanned the dark, trying to locate the voice.

She worked closer to him, softly, until she was sure and then, with a muffled whisper she called his name again.

"C'est Adrienne."

He came toward her, found her, and grasped her hand without saying a word but the strength of his presence killed the fear that had started to rise in her.

Pierre had buried his gear and immediately had tried to find his bearings and make contact with Georges and Adrienne. Now they were together they would look for Georges and plan from there.

But the ground agents?

Pierre felt the same uncomfortable silence that seemed to hang over the field as if the two of them were suspended in a limbo, cut off from all human contact forever. He was now suspiciously peering around into the darkness, trying to judge their approximate position in the field, what might lie at the outer reaches and wondering who might be waiting for them in the shadows and where. As far as he could see there was no moving figure, no sign of Georges or of anyone else.

They started walking. Pierre took Adrienne by the hand and smiled toward her.

"It is better this way. If we are surprised then we are only lovers walking in a field. Right?"

Adrienne smiled back at him and squeezed his hand. Her courage was now strong within her, she had regained her confidence and she was ready to proceed with her mission. They

158

walked quietly, tentatively, across the field, expecting at any moment to meet the looming figure of Georges or of some one of the ground agents.

Suddenly, with no sound, with no warning, they were in a flood of light. As if some giant hand had flipped a silent switch, three enormous searchlights stabbed them with a merciless glare. Adrienne tensed to run but Pierre gripped her with a hand so strong she almost screamed out with pain. He had paused but an instant when the lights went on and now he was proceeding as before, slowly across the field, holding Adrienne by the hand.

So this is how it will be. We will bluff our way out if this is hostile action. If it is friendly, what difference does the glare of light make? She walked beside him, hand in hand, squinting ahead into the blaze of blue-white light until her eyes ached and she longed to call out for darkness. Miles. Was it miles they walked, in the glare of light, or only yards? Yards that seemed like miles, surely, in her tormented terror which couldn't be unleashed because the strong, immediate, felt presence of Pierre held her firm.

He chose to walk directly into one of the lights, slowly, never faltering, never once showing by any outward action the slightest fear, the slightest doubt. Her admiration for his courage gave her her own. The first panic feeling of flight had vanished as quickly as it had come, perhaps because flight was so obviously impossible. The three searchlights were placed in a triangular pattern at the edge of the field and they were pinioned in the cross blaze of the lights.

Still the awful silence. No sound. No voices. No movement of any kind other than their own slow progress across the field cut into the stillness of the night. They were walking hand in hand, eyes cast down against the glare of the light, conscious only of the slowly approaching presence of the enormous illuminating eye. To Adrienne it was as unreal as a nightmare.

"Achtung! HALT!"

159

The two words slashed the silence like a rapier. Pierre squeezed her hand until all feeling left it and they stood rigidly in the field now fifty yards from the huge searing beacon. Everything seemed to come alive at once.

From behind the light, several figures in grey uniforms appeared. Each man was armed, his gun carried rib high at the ready. And then they were engulfed.

Roughly they were pulled apart and quickly searched. Pierre's gun and knife were taken from him. Then, gleefully, they found the small revolver strapped to Adrienne's leg underneath her skirt. They held her skirt high, prodded her indecently and made coarse remarks as they unstrapped the holster. Pierre lunged at them, cursed them and was battered to the ground by a rifle butt, unconscious.

There was a sharp command from the leader of the group, an order to be careful and admonition to remember that these prisoners were to be brought in alive. Then the sound of motors starting and Adrienne saw them drag Pierre's unconscious form out of the light and into the shadows. Moments later, after an exchange of short commands, there was the roar of an accelerating motor, it receded and was gone and there was only the throb of other motors idling and mixture of voices.

Then it was her turn.

Firmly, but without the earlier roughness, she was led to a waiting car. A soldier was already seated in the rear and she was pushed in beside him. Another followed her into the car so that she was seated on the rear seat between two men in uniform. A third slid into the front seat beside the driver. Suddenly the glare of the searchlights vanished and there was a deep woolly darkness as they drove away.

Strangely, she felt no enervating fear. Anger had flared in her at the indecencies of the searching men and the slugging of Pierre had hardened her in a way she had thought impossible. She was in complete command of herself, emotionally,

160

and her strenuous agent training was beginning to work. Instinctively, as the car sped along the road, she tried to orient herself. Every tree, every hillock, every turn of the road, dark as it was, had to be imprinted somehow on her brain. If they had dropped in the area pinpointed for them, and she was sure they had, then Maastricht would be off to the left. But the total blackout of war made any verification impossible. There was no horizon glow anywhere to indicate a town.

A hand slid across her upper leg, glided back and remained still. With a reflex action she slapped the face of the soldier. The result was instantaneous. Everyone started shouting, there was a sudden, sinister, clipped exchange of comment and command and the car was pulled to the side of the road and halted. All of the doors seemed to open at once and in another moment she was dragged from the car, pulled across a ditch and through a hedge row and into a field.

The four men took turns raping her.

Adrienne remembered nothing until she came out of a comatose sleep in a brightly lighted cell. There was nothing in the cell excepting a single bucket to be used as a toilet. No chair, no bed, no blanket, not even straw. And outside, angled from the ceiling so that it flooded her with light, a spotlight played into her cell from the corridor. Her body ached, her mouth was bruised and her hair had been shaved to her scalp. Almost in panic she put both hands to her head and ran her fingers back and forth over the bare smoothness of her skull. Again, and yet again, searching and hoping and yet already knowing that it was gone, she sought the only thing that had stood between her and endless tortures. The tiny cyanide pill which had been hidden close to her scalp, fastened to her hair with a drop of collodion, was gone.

Time meant nothing. She had no idea whether it was still the night of her drop, or the next or the next. Or even if it was night or day. Nor did she have any idea where she was.

161

What had happened to Pierre, or, more puzzling still, what had become of Georges? The fact that she knew nothing of Georges gave her some hope for she felt that he could have escaped, perhaps by overshooting the field in his drop. At least he could alert London to the fact that the mission had aborted.

Then there was the sound of jack-boots on stone, two guards appeared, unlocked her cell and motioned to her to follow them. They went down a narrow, brightly lighted corridor and into a small room at the end. She drew in a quick sob of breath as she saw Pierre. He was standing between two guards, his hands shackled in front of him. His head had been shaved. He spoke her name and smiled and she started to answer but a guard cut her off with a warning that all speech was forbidden except in answer to direct questions from officers.

They waited in silence in the small room. Then there was the sudden clicking of heels as the guards straightened to attention and a young, stiff-backed officer appeared. He exchanged a few words with one of the guards, snapped his head in a gesture of command, turned and opened a door at the opposite side of the room. As he stepped through the door the guards urged Adrienne and Pierre forward and through the door after him.

They stepped into a large, bare, shadowed room with a stone floor, stone walls and barred windows high on the walls. The place stank of must, stale cigarette smoke and dead air, repellent and nauseating. At the far end there were three crude wooden tables placed end to end to form one long counter. Four pads lay at intervals on the tables, there was a chair behind each pad and there was a person seated in each chair. Adrienne glanced at the scene and looked quickly away, not wanting to acknowledge what was before her. But something impelled her to look again.

Three of the four figures were dressed in the field grey uniform of the Nazi trooper and wearing the arrogantly peaked

162

caps of officers. The fourth figure was dressed in civilian clothes and hatless. Adrienne almost screamed her shock.

The fourth figure, seated to the left of the three officers, was Georges. He was staring impassively straight ahead into the room. Pierre had stopped in sudden astonishment when he recognized him, glanced toward Adrienne, spat at the floor and uttered one word under his breath.

"Merde."

Adrienne and Pierre stared at him transfixed as they approached the tables. Georges looked over and beyond them as though they ceased to exist, were invisible, unknown. And then he vanished from their sight along with the three officers behind the blinding barrier of light which suddenly flooded their persons, stabbed into their eyes and blinded them to everything in the hateful room.

The questioning went on and on. It began as a polite query as to who they were, where they had come from and why they were out in a field so late at night. The very politeness of the questions and the manner in which they were phrased gave a sinister quality to the inquiry. The three officers took turns with the drilling, prodding inquisition but the voice they waited and hoped anxiously to hear the way one longs for verification of something too horrible to believe, the voice they knew was there, remained silent. Georges took no part in the cross-examination.

There was a pause. There was a rustling of papers behind the blinding wall of light. A stillness. Then the floodlights faded to a hot glow and were gone. The chairs in front of them were empty, the tables were bare, the guards led them back to their cells.

The Nazi genius for the refinement of torture began to show. Glaring floodlights, twenty-four hours a day, probed at Adrienne until her head reeled with pain, her eyes blurred with fatigue and her whole body ached. Singly and together, at odd intervals and for long stretches, Adrienne and Pierre

163

were taken back to the suffocating room for questioning but they refused to break. Georges had vanished as silently as he appeared for he never again sat in on the interrogations and Adrienne never saw him again.

But now the questioning was taking an uglier turn. There were direct accusations of spying and probing questions concerning the nature of her mission, her contacts, her objectives. Adrienne refused to give, her will was steeled within her and she didn't break. Then, quite suddenly one day in the middle of an interrogation, she was stripped, led into a small bath, immersed in a tub of scalding water, dragged out and pushed into a tub of ice water and then, when the pain was almost beyond endurance, back again to the scalding tub with the questions being shouted, screamed, spattered at her until her head reeled into unconsciousness.

There was a lull, the terrifying sessions stopped, she had no idea for how long but every minute seemed a golden relief. Then, with no explanation, her cell was changed, she was led to another section of the building and found herself in another cell, slightly larger, still bare and still under the cruelty of floodlight but with a difference. There, just across a small corridor, was Pierre.

He smiled at her and winked and her heart felt a sudden lift, a sudden surge of courage but there was a haunted look in his face, he was thin and he was bruised. The significance of the change was soon apparent.

The bully boys now began to question first one and then the other, accompanied with torture. While guards forced Adrienne to the front of her cell facing the cell in which Pierre was being questioned they went to work on him. He was stripped and flogged and she closed her eyes to the horror and stuffed her ears against the crack of the lash. Another day they were back and when they were through, when Pierre's screams had pierced every effort she could make to drown them out, he lay broken, bleeding and gasping on the stone

164

floor. Blood was flowing unchecked from his hands. All of his fingernails had been ripped out.

When her turn came, she was stripped, thrown to the floor and raped in turn by three officers while Pierre was forced to watch. When he closed his eyes and cursed his guards they beat him until he opened them again. And then, when each officer had straightened his clothes and released Adrienne to the next in turn, he turned toward Pierre and spat in his face.

Again the sadists returned to Pierre and this time with the most dreaded of all the Nazi tortures, the electrodes. They were placed in his ears, he was questioned and if the answer was unsatisfactory, the current was applied. The electrodes were placed in his nostrils and pressed again. And they were attached to his testicles and the current turned on. All of this and more, Adrienne was forced to watch. And little by little both of them, Pierre and Adrienne, without knowing it, were slipping into a kind of madness, a stupefaction, where one more horror seemed to be just one more horror and not particularly surprising.

It all stopped as suddenly as it began, almost as if there had been a mistake. Hours seemed to drag by when they saw no one but the guard who brought them the slop that was supposed to be food. How many days, how many nights, no one knew. Certainly neither Adrienne or Pierre.

Nor did she have any idea how many days had passed when they were finally taken out of their cells and driven to another prison. It was in the dark of night and they drove for several hours before they were halted at a barbed wire barricade. Again huge floodlights were suddenly pouring over them as their guards presented credentials. There was a brief argument about letting the car into the grounds, an insistence that the prisoners be made to walk to their quarters. It was resolved and they were driven into the compound, past long rows of dark, unpainted, low barracks. It could have been Buchenwald, Adrienne never knew.

165

Again they were given cells across from one another and again the tortures began. They were made the worse here because now they could hear the screams and shouts of others, persons they never knew or ever saw, sudden shrieks of terror, stabbing screams of pain and then the awful silence of their own solitary confinement.

One day they had come for Pierre and after he had been gone for some time, they came for her. She was led down a long corridor, it was a wooden building, and then outside into a bare, dirt and weed covered square surrounded by more of the low, drab barracks. In the center of the square six heavy poles had been set into the ground and lashed against each pole was the naked body of a man. Sadistically, her guards pointed out to her that one of the men was Pierre. There were others, like herself, flanked by guards and facing the men lashed to the poles and there was a scattered group of officers standing to one side.

While they watched, other men, obviously prisoners from their filthy, tattered, emaciated condition, were taking huge, bloody gobs of raw meat and tying them around the waists of the naked men so that the piece of meat hung over their bodies like a loin cloth. Almost before they had finished their grotesque assignment, a large, coarse featured, blonde woman appeared. She was wearing a uniform, highly polished boots and carried a swagger stick, tucked under one arm. Padding at heel beside her and leashed together with a glistening chain, was a brace of massive black police dogs.

The dogs now became restive, as if anticipating what was to happen. They strained at the leash, raised onto their hind legs against the restraint and whimpered.

The blonde laughed coarsely and then, with a sudden slip of the leash, released the dogs. They raced to the defenseless men standing before them, lunged forward and leapt for the meat. Ripping, tearing, snarling and growling, they tore at the

166

meat, ripped at the men, again and again, until their muzzles were bloody and the men had been brutally emasculated.

Adrienne covered her ears against the screams of the men and the hoarse, maniacal laughter of the woman and she closed her eyes against the horror of the scene. And each time she did so a guard cut her with a whip and commanded her to watch.

Pierre lay for days in festering agony, hoping for death and yet unable to command it. Then, quite suddenly one day when his strength had returned enough, he slugged a guard who brought him food, fought and bit and kicked and scratched and slugged until he was shot in his cell by other guards who had heard the disturbance. They dragged his body out by the feet and left the bloody shambles of his cell for Adrienne to watch.

With Pierre went most of her courage and yet the example of his last fight stirred her to bring about her own destruction. The opportunity came soon and she grasped it. Slyly, and alone, an officer slipped into her cell to assault her. Adrienne turned on him in a fury, kicked, scratched and pummelled him as he fought for possession. His face was close to her as they rolled on the floor and in a last desperate defense she used her teeth. With all her strength she bit into his cheek, felt her teeth meet and felt the sudden gush of blood. It was over. His face bleeding, his cheek ripped open, the officer cursed, struck at her and left.

An hour later they pulled all of her teeth.

Once more Adrienne was moved. It was a longer trip this time and in a closed van crowded to suffocation with men, women and children, too tortured, too wasted to know or care where they were going, where they had been or even who they were. It proved to be her last stop. It was Dachau.

General Donovan had the story. But he didn't have the answer to the question which bothered him. What had hap-

167

pened? What had gone wrong? Was Georges a double agent, in the pay of the Nazis?

A sophisticated guess, one that an informed intelligence operative would perhaps make, was that he was not. Had Georges been a double agent it is doubtful if Adrienne and Pierre would have been captured and tortured. A clever double agent would have permitted them to go on with their mission. He would have let them build their cover, make their contacts, report to London and begin to produce. Then, and only then, would he have moved in, at a time when capture would have paid bigger dividends for the enemy.

And yet how could one explain the floodlights already in position at the drop site? Obviously the Nazis knew a team was coming into the area, otherwise how would they have been ready and waiting?

General Donovan puzzled over all of these questions and more. His reasoning, and the answer which he chose to believe, was based on the assumption of two unrelated factors which must have formed the coincidence that pointed the finger at Georges. Obviously there had been defection on the ground at the drop site. A leak somewhere along the way, among some of the resistance workers, had tipped the Germans off and there had very likely been a fairly extensive clean-up of the group at the last minute. Otherwise, London would surely have been alerted and the mission would have been cancelled. Thus, the Nazis had been tipped and were ready.

The other factor, Georges, could have been simply another German ruse. Georges, fully loyal, could have been captured first and hidden from Adrienne and Pierre. Then, with fiendish cunning, he was presented before the other two at their first questioning in an effort to panic Pierre and Adrienne into full confessions on the assumption that Georges was a double agent. The fact that Georges took no part in the questioning and was never seen again, would bear this out. On the other hand, Georges had a wife and child in enemy territory and he

168

could have been pressured into turning against his teammates after his capture.

General Donovan, and I think others, believed that this had been a strong team which had been betrayed from the ground and not by any one of its members. It is the most sensible and, certainly, the most comforting assumption.

No one will ever know the true story.

It was a full year later, more. The war was long over, General Donovan was back at the practice of law in New York, the OSS had ceased to exist. We lunched together at his apartment on Sutton Place and, as always, we talked of the war, the people in it with us and many related things.

Then he told me.

Only a short time before, he had received the word. Adrienne had survived the catharsis of retelling the horror of her mission. She had gone back to Belgium. Life seemed to be back to normal.

She was found one day hanging from a rod in her clothes closet.

CHAPTER 11

THE FAR EAST—
WITH ONE EYE

THE SECLUDED, secret harbor lay dark and sinister under the sultry night sky. Stretching across limitless miles of the Bay of Bengal to the west lay India, massing the tremendous British effort against the Japanese. And here, on the coast of South Burma, our efforts to gain a strong foothold for an advance were being overwhelmingly repulsed. The irregular Burmese coastline offered hit-and-run haven for the Japanese fleet. It also offered opportunity for infiltration, guerrilla warfare and sabotage.

Unless one knew it was there, unless one had, in bright sunlight, seen the cleverly improvised arrangement of docks and jetties which had converted a former sleepy fishing port

170

into a full-scale service and supply dock, one could easily slip past it in the blackout of the night. Docks, jetties, drydocks, supply warehouses and cranes, they were all there humming with activity under the war-crazed energy of the Japanese. Where once the small fishing boats and trawlers dropped anchor after plying the South Pacific, now injured cruisers of the Japanese Navy, tankers, destroyers, munitions ships, all the water-borne muscle of war, were gathered for yet another hit-and-run blow at the Allied forces in the Far East.

But Han knew it was there. This was Han's own country, the area where he had been born, where he had passed a marginal and yet somehow easy boyhood by the sea. This was where, as an ordinary coolie, he had toiled long days in the little port doing the thousands of small tasks that go to make up the life of an oriental fishing village. The hauling of supplies, the loading and unloading of cargo, the mending of nets, the washing down of ships and the cleaning of fish. This is where there had been those wonderful days when he was free to fish on his own, exploring the favorite fishing grounds, lazing along the coastline, learning and living and drinking in the enjoyment of the life that was hard and yet free, poor and at the same time strangely rich.

Then the hated Japanese had come. Brutally they had taken over the little port, brought in their emergency repair and supply crews and turned the sleepy harbor village into a nightmare. They had good reason. It was a deep harbor, it was protected, isolated and, they hoped, unknown to the enemy. As an auxiliary supply and repair base it saved the time and danger of returning to Japan for repairs for at least nearly all of their surface ships excepting the larger battleships and cruisers.

All of this Han knew.

That was why he was there now sliding silently over the surface of the glossy black water. He was nude, sitting crouched and tense in the bow of the tiny boat, his head turned to one side to listen and to peer into the sullen darkness around him. He was small, compact, muscled and lithe, the perfect human machine for the job ahead. Facing him in the stern was his companion, nude like himself and of the same small hard physique. His hands were on the handle of one long oar which hung over the stern of the little boat and which he worked quickly but silently back and forth with a kind of wriggling motion to propel them forward.

Indonesian? Chinese? Burmese? Who knows? What white man could surely and immediately identify these small men with the black slant-eyes, the lean yellow-tan bodies and the friendly, smiling willingness to sacrifice themselves to the most incredible dangers?

Everything had been made ready before they had pushed off in their little boat, everything arranged so that there would be no need for speech, no need for communication other than the slightest nod of the head or flick of the finger to indicate direction. The boat itself had been designed and built for this very purpose, just large enough for the two men. It was flat of bottom and light enough to skim across the surface of the water like those incredible small insects which dart across ponds and lakes without leaving the trace of a ripple, without causing the slightest hiss of sound. A tiny pontoon hung out to each side to keep the boat from capsizing when someone left it or entered it from the water.

They were getting in closer now for they could hear the occasional voice and the low hum of generators and machinery indicating that the Japs were at work, as usual, around the clock. Now the chatter of a drill, the hammer of a riveter, the hiss of steam, it was all there in the gloom of the blackout. There was the occasional, sudden glow of light as a door opened and closed in the distance. It was made the brighter by the blackness around them and the double pattern of the reflection in the water. Otherwise everything was darkness. The Japanese were clever enough not to risk the flare of an

172

acetylene torch or other flame at night. That work they reserved for the daylight hours.

Han was anxiously watching, squinting his already slanted eyes until they almost ceased to exist, looking for the darker outline of a hull. Nervously, quickly, he felt over the straps and buckles which held the flippers to his feet, the long, black, rubber fins like the exaggerated web of a duck's foot. They would give him the added thrust and speed he would need once he was under the water.

The oarsman, still wriggling his pole, was straining to peer ahead into the dark looking for his quarry. It didn't have to be a specific target, they knew, but it was always nice to pick something big. It made a bigger splash.

Another quick flash and fade of light illumined the stern of a large ship just ahead and a trifle to the right. It was perhaps a hundred yards away. But they were unable to tell, in the quick glow, what class of ship it was.

Han was now quietly and calmly busying himself with his limpet. This was the chillingly clever invention of some genius in the British service to be used in the sabotage of shipping. Named after the small sea creature that attaches itself to rocks and underwater surfaces by means of suction, the limpet was a magnetized explosive charge that could be placed against the hull of a ship to blow it up. About the size of an ordinary brick, the device carried a timing mechanism that could be activated to go off some time after it had been put in place allowing the saboteur ample time for escape.

Han strapped the limpet around his waist, secured against his body to give him the ultimate in freedom once he was in the water and yet easily accessible when he wanted it. He did it all quickly, surely and with practiced skill. The oarsman's eyes were steadily watching him now with only an occasional glance ahead into the dark. He watched as Han fastened a length of black fishing line to his waist, drew it snug to the

173

little reel that was fastened inboard against the side of the tiny boat and then again felt the adjustment of his flippers.

They were skimming more slowly now, almost drifting on the surface of the water. Everything was black around them, black and still with only the muffled activity of the docks in the background to keep them in touch with reality. Then, so near it almost startled them into exclamation, there was the quiet, gentle but unmistakable slap of water against a hull and they knew they were in close. Close enough.

Now they could see it, the looming hull of a ship, a blacker form in the black night. They were almost under the flare of a wide, low stern but they could distinguish nothing other than the great bulk of the dark ship.

Han judged his distance, made a quickly silent sign to his companion and grasped the side of the boat. With a slow, sinuous motion, like a gymnast raising his body to a hand stand, Han lifted his small form and slid it over the side of the boat. It tilted until the little pontoon rested on the water. Then, as his body slipped softly into the sea, Han slowly and cautiously released the weight of his body from the side of the small craft. The pontoon lifted from the water without a sound and the little boat was once more on an even keel with the oarsman steadying it at the stern.

He rested for a moment in the water beside the boat, filling his lungs for the ordeal ahead of him, getting his bearings. In another moment his head disappeared silently below the surface and he was gone. He swam rapidly, found the steel plates of the hull well below the water line and reached for his limpet. It released quickly to his pull and almost jumped from his hand as the steel plates of the ship reacted to the magnet. Han felt the limpet jam solidly against the side of the ship, gave it a tap to assure himself it would hold and then let his body float to the surface.

Snugged close against the side of the ship, he waited a moment to get his breath. Then, as silently as before, he sank beneath the surface. As he did so he tugged on the black fishing line secured to his waist and felt the reassuring answer as his companion held the tension. With the tautened line as a guide he made his way swiftly back to the small boat waiting for him. In another moment he surfaced silently beside the small craft and peered up into the beaming face of his oarsman.

He was breathing heavily, partly from his exertion, partly from excitement and he clung to the side of the boat for a few seconds to get his lungs filled. Then, almost imperceptibly, with magnificent body control, he gradually pressed his weight down on his hands, slowly, until the little pontoon had silently touched against the water. In another instant he had slithered into the boat controlling the placement of his body weight until the pontoon had lifted again and the craft had righted itself.

The oarsman had now started his wriggling motion with the long oar and they were under way. Han lay in the bottom of the boat, closed his eyes and breathed deeply of the heavy, warm, humid night air. Only half consciously was he aware of the occasional sudden glow from the shipyard, the receding hum of the activity that, only a short time ago, had seemed so important to him. He lay in the darkness and dozed. Now there was more motion to the little boat and he knew they were out of the quiet water of the hidden harbor, working along the shore line back to the base from which they had started.

The concussion nearly lifted their small boat out of the water. There was a sudden feeling of tremendous pressure, a sort of sucking in and blowing out, all in one motion, of the heavy air around them and then the heavy, crashing boom of an explosion. With it there was a brilliant flare of light, bright as day, and then ebbing to a reddish glow.

Han sat up quickly in the boat, looked at the oarsman facing him and smiled. His companion smiled back at him and worked his long oar faster in a kind of exultation.

175

Han was about to speak when it happened. There was another tremendous concussion, a roaring explosion, then another and another in quick succession. The next moment the sky was bright, growing brighter and brighter with a yellow-red leaping flare of light. A siren shrieked into the night and suddenly all was madness. Flame. Explosion. A short series of staccato bursts like a huge chain of firecrackers going off. The ever growing hideousness of the flame and the now billowing clouds of black oil smoke.

Everything around them was bright as day and they knew that, if they could see around the jutting point of land that separated them from the secret harbor they would be able to see the running figures, the silhouetted figures of the ships, the leaping flames and the huge, rolling, enveloping clouds of oily black smoke. As it was they revelled in the holocaust as it burst over the line of trees that separated them from their target.

For one impetuous moment Han was overwhelmed with a suicidal desire to turn back, to get a really first-hand view of the havoc he had implemented. But the thoroughness of his training prevented him from giving in to a whim that he knew could mean only one thing. He sat silently in the boat and watched the brilliance of the sky, listened to the sirens and the roaring of the flames. It was maddening not to know exactly what one had accomplished.

A munitions ship? Perhaps. A tanker? Again perhaps. The fantastic possibility of two, one touching off the other? Just possible. But he would never know. He would only know that he had accomplished another mission for OSS. He would only know that the long, gruelling, tedious hours of training that he had endured, along with others like him, had paid off.

In this particular instance it had paid off rather handsomely.

Somewhere, hidden in the background history of the U.S. war effort in the Far East, there is a chapter on inter-service politics and rivalry that is not attractive. How it all started, on what it devolved, from what it stemmed, it would be safe to assume only a few persons in the higher echelons ever knew. There will be no attempt here to understand, study, or explain it. There will be only the recording of it.

That chapter concerns the adamant, unreasoned and continued refusal of General Douglas MacArthur to permit the OSS to operate anywhere under his command. Despite the proven effectiveness of the OSS operations in North Africa, Italy, the Balkans, France, Germany, the Scandinavian countries, and the neutral areas, General MacArthur insisted that under his command the only intelligence functions would be carried out by his own army G.2. It was somewhat akin to a man with failing eyesight refusing to get new glasses or, in this instance, using a magnifying glass. As General Donovan so aptly phrased it, "We were allowed to operate in the Far East with only one eye."

Of course the scuttlebutt was voluminous. Some said that General MacArthur, as an old-line West Pointer and believer in the chain of command, refused to have any autonomous agency functioning within his sphere. With General Donovan answerable only and directly to President Roosevelt, he felt his own effectiveness would be weakened. It seemed to carry no weight with him that OSS was functioning effectively and without friction in all other commands.

Whatever it was, the fact remained that OSS did not, at any time, have operatives or missions functioning within the area under General MacArthur's jurisdiction.

If one thought that would keep the OSS out of the Far East as an effective and hard-hitting espionage and sabotage organization, he was basing his thinking on premises that showed a complete innocence of the Donovan drive and persistence. It also showed a lack of understanding of General Donovan as a patriot and a civilian-military figure in the finest sense of the term.

177

General Donovan had dreamed up OSS. He had built that dream into the most forceful, efficient and effective implement for espionage and sabotage that this country has ever seen. It began as a civilian organization and only because of increasing war pressures within the operating theaters did it become a quasi-military organization. Although Donovan himself had seen war service in the first World War, he was at heart a civilian and he continued to operate as such even while dressed in an officer's uniform and wearing the two stars of a Major General. Rank meant nothing to him. That was borne out on more than one occasion within the OSS. In my own case it was most sharply defined when he issued a directive to all personnel stating that, although the Special Funds Officer was ranked below some of the branch personnel, he would take no orders from any ranking officers other than Colonel Bruce and General Donovan. It was in this same vein of thought that he quite properly felt he had no obligation whatsoever to observe General MacArthur's edict. OSS had a vital service to offer, a vital function to perform. General Donovan, with the full consent of the President, moved into the Pacific. It is to his credit that he scrupulously observed the MacArthur wishes within his own domain.

It is a sad commentary on the MacArthur intransigence that OSS first appeared in the South Pacific area under the aegis of Lord Mountbatten of the British Naval Service. OSS bases were established in New Delhi, Calcutta and Karachi in India. An OSS base was established in Ceylon, a Shangri-La type of establishment where the purpose of the mission seemed the more sinister against the languid tropical beauty of the setting. General Orde Wingate of the British Army cooperated and worked closely with the OSS establishments, and soon we were in Burma, then far away in the northeast corner of Assam. From there it was a natural progression into Kunming and eventually into Chunking with the cooperation of General

Stilwell, the famous "Vinegar Joe" of the U.S. services. By a circuitous route we had made it.

The pattern was similar to that which had developed in North Africa and the European Theater of operations. Training areas were established where personnel were instructed in the techniques of sabotage and espionage. Here, perhaps more than in any other area, the training approximated that of guerrilla warfare with emphasis on jungle fighting under the most desperate conditions. Natives were recruited and trained with telling effect both for the purpose of infiltrating enemy territory to gather intelligence and for the wider range of organizing resistance fighters and saboteurs.

From an isolated area in northern Assam sabotage and resistance supplies of every description were flown over the "hump" to our operatives. The pressure was stepped up. Enemy supply depots were destroyed, lines of communication were cut, relentlessly the Japs were pushed back out of the area, harassed, demoralized, and surprised.

The British services were cooperative to the fullest extent. Perhaps because of the incredible problems presented by the Far Eastern operations it became essential that no wasted double effort be permitted. The length of the Malay Peninsula, Burma, Thailand, Indonesia, Assam—the terrain was formidable, the lack of adequate roads and other communication frustrating, the climate appalling. Add to that the fact that we, as whites, were immediately identifiable, and the complexities of operating clandestine missions should be obvious. Where, within enemy-occupied Europe, we had been able to infiltrate our own people disguised as natives to organize and support sabotage projects, in the China, Burma area it was necessary to school native organizers to handle the on-the-spot operations. The fact that they were effective proved the ingenuity and persistence of our Far Eastern units.

Because of the vast importance of shipping to the Japanese war effort, OSS trained and used innumerable underwater

179

sabotage teams to accomplish the type of mission so successfully carried out by the young agent, Han. We organized and infiltrated special units to ferret out and destroy Japanese munitions dumps, supply depots and communications centers, always utilizing native personnel with the American organizers staying in the background to equip and train ever more teams. Our natives were adept. And they were daring.

One young Chinese discovered a small, under-guarded Japanese field prison camp and volunteered to liberate it. He tunnelled his way into the compound and made contact with the surprised prisoners. The escape of a few via his tunnel would assure reprisals and torture for those left behind. He sought to save all with a mass escape. He agreed to bring in small arms, ammunition, and grenades enough to overpower the Japanese guards and free everyone. OSS supplied the weapons.

For several consecutive nights, he and two equally cool and daring accomplices made trips through the tunnel, carefully burying the arms and ammunitions within the compound. In a matter of minutes one bright morning during the exercise period, he made his appearance, armed the prisoners and spurred them to action. They killed their guards, blasted the flimsy buildings of the compound to splinters and were free. By the time the nearest Japanese garrison was aware of what had happened some two hundred former prisoners had melted into the countryside as if they had never existed. Our man brought back several new recruits for OSS with him.

As we found elsewhere, the women were as selfless and as daring as the men. There was the young Indonesian girl who attached herself to a Japanese officer and became a part of his retinue. She sent us back information through cut-outs and then, when she had reason to believe that she was becoming suspect, she developed a new angle to the use for the cyanide pill with which she had been provided. Instead of using it herself, she slipped it to the Japanese officer. It was a tribute to her cunning that she got away with it and continued to keep us informed of Japanese military schemes through other contacts she had made.

Kunming, with its thousands of refugees, its soldiers and Allied airmen, had much the atmosphere of a frontier town in pioneer days. It was gold for OSS. By the careful screening of every possible type and kind of person we were able to gain valuable background information on the Japanese military position. It proved to be a never-failing reservoir for agent recruits and by their training and use we were able to step up the harassment of sabotage and guerrilla warfare.

Even the children got into the act in the Far East. With the determination to leave nothing untried our Research and Development division came up with a particularly unattractive way to demoralize the Japanese. Through the Far Eastern cultures section in Washington they had discovered that the Japanese are especially fastidious with regard to the bodily functions. Working on this thesis and aware of the strict officer code within the Japanese military, a disgusting soft paste with the strong odor of human excrement was created, packaged into squeeze tubes and sent into areas occupied by Japanese troops. It was a simple matter to get the Japanese-hating residents, especially the children, to squirt this revolting stuff onto the clothing of any passing Japanese uniform. If it caused loss of face, if it created embarrassment, if it crushed pride only for a moment, it was one more small thorn in the enemy flesh. Somewhat facetiously the product was called by the idea boys in Washington "Who, Me?"

So it went. Every day brought new stories of heroism, new deeds of daring, new sacrifices. And each one was more fantastic than the last. Like the agent who preferred to sacrifice his own life rather than to run for safety and endanger the lives of his teammates, thereby causing the failure of their mission. It was his death that assured the successful completion of their assignment. Or the one who elected to go forward

181

to meet capture and certain torture in order to gain the vital added moments necessary for his companions to accomplish the intelligence mission in the midst of which they had been surprised. Such things became so commonplace they were only noted in passing in the tension and pressure of the conflict, almost as if they were to be expected and accepted as normal. Sudden bright flames of incredible selflessness and heroism, marked, but not long remembered. And if remembered, only by the few to whom the person may have been a code number, certainly a code name. Faceless, unnamed, unknown heroes of the loneliest kind of warfare, the secret warfare of espionage.

This very record became a vindication of the Donovan vision and persistence. That the OSS operations within the Burma, India, China theater contributed considerably to the over-all success of the Allied forces in the Far East has been officially acknowledged on more than one occasion. That it was as effective, done, as General Donovan said, "with only one eye," makes the accomplishment all the more remarkable.

How much more could have been accomplished, what the over-all picture would have been had General MacArthur permitted the use of the other eye, no one can begin to guess. It is something that will be argued within the higher, secret inner sanctum of war and politics as long as there are military strategists to give it thought.

CHAPTER 12

THE MAZE

THE Office of Strategic Services and the original organization from which it derived, the Office of the Co-ordinator of Information, began as a civilian agency of the U.S. Government. That was in October, 1941. Before the creation of the Central Intelligence Agency in 1947, the last vestige of the outfit withered on the vine as the Strategic Services Unit of the War Department. Certainly in concept it would have perhaps been preferable had the organization gone through the entire World War II as a civilian agency. General Donovan favored the civilian concept as did President Roosevelt; and they both, especially General Donovan, did everything possible to retain the civilian stamp on the vast complex. It is doubtful, in retrospect, if anyone could have prevented the gradual militarization that took place.

There were many who felt that General Donovan made the first mistake when he went back into active service himself and put on a uniform. They felt that that was the opening wedge for military direction and control. And perhaps it would have eliminated many later problems had the General remained a civilian and a high-priority blanket exemption from military service had been granted all agency personnel. At best one can only speculate.

The encroachment by the military was gradual and at first imperceptible. There was the occasional reaching out on the part of OSS and plucking someone already in one of the services for duty within the OSS. Then, as more young, draft-eligible employees within the organization felt the hot breath of the armed services on their necks the OSS arranged for them to be assigned back to their regular civilian spot in the agency. Little by little, from both angles, more Army and Navy uniforms made their appearance.

The whole process was given tremendous impetus as OSS opened forward bases within the war theaters. Beginning with outposts in Casablanca, Algiers and Cairo the emphasis was on the military. Not that we couldn't have continued to operate with a full civilian roster. It was quite simply that, from a housekeeping, transportation, and therefore security standpoint, it was simpler and more efficient to meet military requirements. The only possible way to get into a war zone was through Army, Navy, or Air Corps transportation and they were not set up to cater to civilians. In the few instances where OSS found it necessary to insist on the carrying of civilians by service means, the security and cover of the persons involved was so seriously compromised that it hampered the effectiveness of the mission. In short it became obvious that OSS could best operate in a twilight zone, autonomous, semi-civilian, semi-military.

The problems were especially complex in the early days before the organization became known to the various military and naval commands. Independently established OSS headquarters, such as those in Algiers and Casablanca, operated separately and apart from the regular Allied commands. However, as the need for more and varied sabotage units grew, it was apparent that their efficiency could be increased by the use of already available service facilities. Especially with regard to rations and fuel, it was soon evident that the Army and Navy supply stores would have to be used. This brought more direct contact. This brought cooperation. Eventually it brought everything but absorption.

This was only one facet of the problem, however. General Donovan's conception of the OSS was as an organization all-encompassing in its knowledge—and its services. As he so often stated, "The Office of Strategic Services means just that, services, of a strategic nature, in every category, for the use of the Army, Navy and Air Corps." If the production of that service meant a semi-absorption by the larger body then, within the limits of efficiency and security, he was ready to accept it.

From the outset the growth and development of the organization had been played by ear. Research and Analysis to produce the background material in every possible field and area from European history, economic and social and political, to Far Eastern cultures. Special Intelligence to gather specific information from within enemy territory. Special Operations to carry out sabotage within enemy territory. X2 to handle counterintelligence. Morale Operations for the dissemination of black propaganda. Communications to develop and direct clandestine transmitters. Field Photographic to handle photographic reconnaissance and intelligence. Research and Development to create special weapons and devices. Special Documents to forge papers and related items. And Special Funds to finance all espionage and sabotage operations of whatever nature. To service all of this vast collection of branches was an Administrative Services and Transportation branch.

That was the skeleton. From a main Washington base with two other continental bases, one in New York and one in San Francisco, the huge net was directed. Each branch was represented in each war theater and it was there that the meat was put on the skeleton. Casablanca, Marrakech, Rabat, Algiers, Oran, Tunis and Alexandria and Cairo. There were OSS operational bases in them all. And hidden in out-of-the-way villas, small compounds and isolated training areas were innumerable other secret installations for the furtherance of our work. Lisbon, Estoril and Cintra. Madrid, Barcelona, Malaga and San Sebastian. More OSS bases fed by more hidden, isolated nests of activity. Sicily. Sardinia. Corsica. Capri. Bari, Caserta, Sienna, Naples, Rome, Milan, more OSS activity again fed and strengthened by smaller, clandestine outposts. Istanbul. Baghdad. Abadan.

From the moment of D-Day, the OSS had operating bases in France, moving with the Allied forces. St. Lo. St. Pair. Grandville. Ste. Mere Église. Paris, a forward base headquarters, soon was serving outposts at Dijon, Toulouse, Perpignan, Marseilles, Nice and Annemasse. And these in turn had their hidden satellites for the control of agents.

There was of course Bern, with feelers into the heart of Germany and probing into Austria, Hungary, Romania, Czechoslovakia and Yugoslavia. There was Stockholm. And in the Low Countries there were OSS bases in Copenhagen, Eindhoven, Maastricht, Antwerp and Brussels with still more secret villas adding their bit to the over-all picture.

In the Far East there was Karachi, New Delhi and Calcutta in India, each with satellite cells. There was Kandy and Colombo in Ceylon. There was Kunming and Chungking with innumerable smaller installations in China. There was Rangoon in Burma with way stations. And there were bases and hideouts in Thailand and Assam. They were all working and operating bases from which smaller, hidden cells were being directed, intertwined, intermeshed in such a way that the greatest possible good could be gained from the smallest mote of information or activity.

It would be almost impossible to say with any certainty how many agents OSS put into the field during the War. The problem is complicated by the fact that we might start with one bona fide agent dispatched from a headquarters base with instructions to feed specific information back. In the gathering of that information such agent could and would conceivably employ several sub-agents of whom we at headquarters would have no exact knowledge. These sub-agents might or might not know they were working for OSS, most likely the latter case being true, but they would nevertheless be agents of the organization in every real meaning of the word. Just as our single agent Duval eventually organized and placed in the field against the enemy nearly seven thousand resistance fighters, "agents" if you will, just so other agents, espionage operatives, recruited and "ran" sub-agents within their respective areas for our purposes. However, from the knowledge we have of agent financing, it would be safe to estimate that OSS had, world-wide, between three and four thousand agents in the field at the height of the war. That figure would of course exclude groups like Duval's resistance forces and other OSS organized, equipped and financed partisan groups.

In England, perhaps more than in any other area, the OSS became more military in its operations. The training areas were many and varied, scattered from the very north of Scotland to the south of England. There were parachute schools, sabotage schools, glider schools and training areas. There were dispatch bases for the sending and receiving of agents. There were rest areas for returned agent personnel and there were commando schools.

It was from England that OSS prepared and dispatched

187

those units that General Donovan saw as being of infinite value to the Allied forces on D-Day and thereafter. Whereas we had been previously concentrating on the small espionage and sabotage team which we continued to utilize to the very end of the war, it was foreseen that OSS could perform another type of service in support of regular troops. The Operational Groups and the Jedburgh Teams were the result.

The Operational Groups, called the OGs for short, were commando-type, guerrilla-trained units. Each unit was to be specially trained for a specific area with the idea that, as the regular forces advanced through France and into Germany, the OGs would be dropped just ahead of our own troops and behind enemy lines. It was a daring and dramatic type of maneuver and it was effective. OG groups might be assigned the task of parachuting into an area to take and hold and prevent the destruction by the enemy of a key power plant, a rail center or a bridge. The whole operation was military from start to finish. The OGs were military personnel, they were attached to a regular unit for their operation and they were directed from that unit. The OSS function was to train, equip and ready them for the work. And they functioned as effectively in the Far East.

The Jedburgh Teams were a joint American and British operation, handled on a fifty-fifty basis. The Jeds, as they were called, were again military personnel put through a rigorous course of special training that fitted them not only to carry on a regular small-scale military operation as an independent unit but also trained and fitted them to organize and train resistance fighters for the same purpose. Some of these teams were large for a drop group, one operation involving ninety men, but for the most part they were held to smaller units for security and command reasons.

Both of these concepts grew out of the progress of the war and were implemented by General Donovan's ingenuity in supplying "strategic services" for the use of regular military, naval

188

or air operations. They were only a fractional part of the picture.

The roster of services was staggering. Voluminous, detailed and updated reports were available on any segment of any area of the world. They formed the background material for the briefing of the President in his high level talks, for the use of military, naval and air commanders in the field and for the Nuremberg trials. High-grade, top secret intelligence from the very heart of enemy territory, that, too, was available. The most ingenious, cunning and successful sabotage operations. The running and control of double agents. Special radio devices, miniature cameras, special weapons, these, too, were available. Clothing, documents, passports, ticket stubs, ration cards, foreign equipment of any and every kind, suitable to any type of operation, proper for any part of the world, these were created by OSS.

Billets, messes, independent communications and special transportation, all these were operated and maintained by OSS for increased efficiency and security of operation. It was a world of its own and as varied. There was the chateau in France used as an OSS base where the owner still lived under house arrest as a collaborator. And while the clandestine missions of OSS seethed around him he was permitted the limited enjoyment of his garden. Twice a day the gentleman, his wife and two children made a tour of the estate. But because there were many mosquitoes and biting flies in the area, their excursion was made under a huge netting stretched over a bamboo frame built onto bicycle wheels. With the family safely under the netting a liveried footman wheeled the strange contraption around the garden. He was not protected from the insects.

There was the beautifully remote tea plantation in Assam where the tranquillity of the area belied the tremendous activity involved in supplying all of the hideously ingenious devices of sabotage. And there were the sprawling country estates in England where the once manicured gardens had become

189

obstacle courses for the training of agents. Whether the setting was a villa in Algiers, an old palace in Italy, a plantation in Ceylon or a town house in Stockholm, the pattern was the same. There was an urgency to produce the ultimate in information, to further in every possible way the Allied effort against the Axis.

General Donovan moved through the maze with the familiar assurance of a spider on his web. Every new device, every new pattern, every new area simply enlarged the scope and efficiency of the OSS as a service organization on the highest level. It would not seem humanly possible to understand and administer such a varied and widespread empire. Yet those who grew with the organization from the start seemed to see no chaos or incoherence. Rather, like General Donovan, they recognized only the natural, inspired and aggressive development of a dream.

To direct such a maze with clear lines of command and full authority was a tremendous challenge. To do it on a quasi-military basis, as was necessary, was a nightmare. It was one thing to say that General Donovan was answerable only and directly to President Roosevelt. It was another thing to make that independence real in the field when up against an aggressive military command. It is a tribute to General Donovan's skill as a diplomat and an operating realist that he was able to steer OSS on a course that kept its autonomy throughout the war under the most tremendous stress.

On first-name terms with the great throughout the world, he was able to utilize that fact when the chips were down and there was a real threat to his independence. Certainly the great cooperation enjoyed between OSS and its opposite British services stemmed in great part from General Donovan's friendship with Prime Minister Churchill, one that long predated the war. The fact that he had direct access to almost anyone anywhere in the world was enhanced by the fact that, in turn, he was reporting, in the final analysis, only to the President.

Thus, though the "alarums and excursions" were numerous and frequent, the problems were invariably solved in favor of OSS autonomy. There was one moment, in the middle of the war, when the Inspector General's office of the War Department moved to make inquiries into certain OSS operating procedures within the ETO. It was quickly and quietly told it had no jurisdiction. There were occasions in the field when Army commanders challenged the freedom of action of OSS units and personnel. They were, again, deftly briefed on the line of authority that permitted such action. And there were times when, with some bewilderment, air-transport despatchers found it necessary to give a captain priority over a colonel on a flight.

Although throughout the war the Washington office of the OSS remained predominantly civilian in character, the outposts became increasingly militarized. And if the militarization was not in reality complete, in the war zone it appeared to be. Once our troops were in France and a base had been established in Paris it was ruled by the military that all civilians should wear a uniform in order to distinguish them from the native population in the war zone. The result was that those persons who moved forward with OSS into France as civilians wore an army type of uniform without insignia. It made the effect complete.

At its peak strength the Office of Strategic Services numbered nearly thirty thousand persons on its roster, spread around the world. With the German surrender the dissolution began and by the time of the Japanese surrender it was a fast dwindling organization.

From the start President Roosevelt had been fascinated with the operations of OSS. As a sophisticated politician and statesman he was well aware of the huge head start the British had on us in the field of intelligence, the result of decades of the most astute operation of clandestine nets throughout the world. He was also aware of our woeful ignorance of the true picture within pre-war Nazi Germany and other important areas of the world. It was only natural that, when General Donovan came up with his blueprint of the organization which was to become the Office of Strategic Services, the President should recognize the need.

Under President Roosevelt, General Donovan had a free hand, ample funds and unlimited authority in the espionage and sabotage field. This was all basic to success. But he had as well the complete confidence of the President.

Under President Truman the rapport was less noticeable. President Roosevelt had consistently refused to assist the War and Navy Departments in their repeated attempts to invade the OSS field or trim its scope. He recognized the value of the independence of the agency and he saw that it was preserved. President Truman, on the other hand, perhaps because he had not seen the origins and growth of the organization at first hand, listened to the service arguments. Espionage and sabotage were war activities, so the Army and Navy argued, and as such they should be under the control of the military. President Truman was inclined to agree.

The first inkling of a concerted move on the part of the Army to take over the OSS came soon after the Japanese surrender. General Donovan met the threat head on. He argued his wellfounded belief in the need for a continued service for the gathering of intelligence, even in time of peace. In an unsettled postwar world, he argued, it was of paramount importance to the security of our country. He insisted, as always, that that service should be an independent agency of the Government. He pointed out the desirability of maintaining it as a civilian operation.

All of these points were made again and again before the Joint Chiefs of Staff, before various investigating committees of top brass from the Army, the Navy and the Air Corps, before members of Congressional Committees. There were whole weeks of conferences at the highest level in Washington during the late summer and early fall of 1945 concerning the eventual fate of the Office of Strategic Services. Over and over again, until the repetition was monotonous, General Donovan argued for the continuance of an independent, civilian, peace-time organization for the gathering of intelligence.

No one can understand, fathom or discover the hundreds of small, almost unrelated factors which go to make up a final decision of the Government in Washington. Certainly, in a matter of the vast importance of a peace-time intelligence network, it would be impossible to consider and weigh every factor. Service rivalries, personalities, power politics, prestige. Anyone would have to be incredibly naïve not to recognize that they all play a part in the most major as well as lesser decisions. They most probably entered into the discussions with regard to the eventual disposition of the OSS.

Throughout the endless conferences General Donovan had insisted that he was interested only in the preservation of the intelligence advantage that the existence of OSS had given the country. He was not, and he repeated it many times, interested in continuing as the head of whatever successor organization the President chose to create. Any charge that he was building a personal power organization of vast scope should have been killed with these avowals. To add emphasis to his sincerity and in the belief that, as one no longer directly affiliated with the organization, he could perhaps carry more weight in the creation of the agency he felt the country so urgently needed, General Donovan tendered his resignation. He returned to civilian life, a private citizen, but with the weight of tremendous experience in the field of espionage behind him. In this capacity he continued to offer his advice and counsel to the embattled conferees involved in the decisions then being taken.

It was a mistake. Where once he had held the power to make decisions, to give advice and be heard, he was now on the sidelines, a private citizen whose warnings could be ignored.

With General Donovan's retirement the military moved in.

193

To those within the organization who had seen the scope and value of the work it had accomplished, the sudden, uninformed take over by the War Department was shockingly short-sighted. An endless succession of Army and Navy brass filed through the organization "observing," questioning, probing. Representatives of the Joint Chiefs of Staff spent long hours questioning key personnel remaining with the agency. The object of the interrogation was announced as an attempt to evaluate the advisability of continuing the Office of Strategic Services as an independent espionage organization in time of peace.

From the tenor of the questioning it was obvious that the situation had been prejudged and the decision already made. Every query, every angle of approach was made to put the OSS on the defensive, to make it justify itself as a continuing operation when the record so glaringly proved the answer. One especially long conference of interrogation which dealt primarily with the use of secret funds proved to be especially weighted in favor of dissolution of the OSS. Why, in time of peace, the questioning went, should it be necessary to maintain a secret and expensive espionage network? The answer given by the OSS officer being queried was direct and to the point.

"Because," he replied, "one should recognize the fact that in time of war we have allies. In time of peace, we have no friends."

It may have been a statement with a slightly cynical tone but certainly it was one made on long and practical experience in espionage. It might even be said that the years since that June of 1946 have given the statement more pertinence.

It was a sad closing to a brief but brilliant chapter in the history of the United States in World War II. For short periods of time new faces topped the roster, now an old line West Point Colonel to whom intelligence was only a word, now a Naval officer with no background understanding of the organization, another and yet another. Almost by the month the command changed and with it the name of the organization. The Office of Strategic Services ceased to exist and in its place was the Strategic Services Unit of the War Department. That in turn gave way to the Central Intelligence Group, still within the War Department.

Finally, there was nothing.

President Truman, with complete lack of sophistication, reacted as if espionage were something one shouldn't speak about, like syphilis in the family. In the meantime the Army and the Navy hardly knew what to do with an organization as unorthodox as OSS. It was simpler to let it die and go back to the safety, organizationally speaking, of G.2 and ONI! Highly trained, widely experienced and loyally dedicated personnel drifted away in dismay and disgust to be lost forever to the country in a sphere of vast importance.

The tragedy behind this action is the more real because of the positive steps General Donovan had taken to guide the Government into avoiding such an error. With the vision that had characterized his development of OSS, General Donovan had, before leaving the organization, made provision for the future of espionage in our country's way of life. Through both government and private means he had indicated the need for a long-range, built-in espionage network. He saw the post-war years as periods of confusion and readjustment affording the perfect opportunity to establish such networks. We were everywhere already, he argued, and it was only wisdom and good policy to dig in, quietly and efficiently, for the long pull. Overseas branches of large corporations, the expanding business picture, the rebuilding of war areas, Government programs for economic, social and health aid to foreign lands, all these were made to order for the infiltration of espionage agents. General Donovan eagerly and realistically presented his arguments for moving the OSS espionage operations into a peace-time program.

Only after the damage had been done, only after the whole

195

vast mechanism had disintegrated, the personnel retired and the void been created, was it realized that espionage was here to stay, like it or not. Washington at last awakened to the truth of what General Donovan had been trying to impress on the proper authorities.

Six months after the dissolution of the Office of Strategic Services, and with infinitely greater effort and expense than would have been necessary had the OSS been preserved, our Government was back in the business of espionage. It was taken out of the hands of the military. It was devoid of any service influence. The new agency was to be a civilian operation as was its earlier parent. The Central Intelligence Agency took over where the OSS had left off.

The man who was picked to head it was Rear Admiral Roscoe Hillenkoetter. He was succeeded by Gen. Walter Bedell Smith. His successor, the first civilian director, was General Donovan's OSS war-time Chief of Mission in Switzerland, Allen W. Dulles.

CHAPTER 13

SUTTON PLACE

THE view over the East River from General Donovan's apartment on Sutton Place was magnificent. High enough, remote enough from the harshness of the grime, the noise and the litter one knew could be found along the river front, there was an unreality about the scene that gave it the drama of a stage set. And whether it was over a seven-thirty breakfast with the sun gilding the room and sparkling the silver, at lunch with the family or sitting late in the evening alone with the General and watching the changing pattern of lights, the conversation was always interesting and often brilliant. It invariably turned, at some time, back to OSS and the war.

Under these circumstances I saw General Donovan at his

197

best. Relaxed as he had never been during the war, unhurried, warmly concerned with the issues at hand, he was still the dynamic, inquiring, imaginative and driving personality. His interest lay everywhere and his reading to feed that interest was prodigious as it had been even throughout the strains of war. It had always fascinated and astonished me, this hungry need for more and more knowledge, more and wider information. On every plane, in every room he occupied during the war there were the piles of books, their leaves parted with markers, their margins pencilled with notations, their words heavily underlined in pertinent places.

Sutton Place was the same.

And like the books that fed it, his brain was marked with quotations, filled with notations and underlined with ideas. He was back now at his law practice, and his daily schedule was staggering, but there was no rest for the mind. Or perhaps the secret was that his relaxation was in his mind, in the ever-inquiring challenge of new ideas, new plans, new problems.

He was disappointed, of course, by the dissolution of the dynamic, aggressive organization he had so energetically created and directed. But he was not bitter. Like an indulgent father making allowances for a wayward son, he understood the human factors behind the decisions that were taken. It was almost as if he had known from the start, known when the organization was first created back in 1941, that this would be its fate, this would be the ending.

Other, vastly more important factors, were of more concern to him. Those factors had to do with some of our personnel. With his usual vision he had foreseen problems in the rehabilitation of agents trained to kill, men trained to destroy, to maim, to burn, pillage and demolish. How, he had asked, did one re-train these men for peaceful living? How did one reverse the process we had been pursuing so avidly for the past four years? How did one teach that that which we had urged and advocated was now wrong, immoral and anti-social?

198

We had brought out all of the jungle instincts in these men. We had schooled them in craft, deceit and stealth. We had trained them to the highest possible pitch of physical and mental keenness for these dread purposes. We had put weapons in their hands, in many cases specially designed weapons to facilitate silent killing, and taught them how best to use them. Then we had sent them out to do our bidding with morale at its peak and the assurance that what they were doing was high heroism. And so it was.

The majority of them, perhaps, would return to normal life with relative ease, leaving the war behind like some unlived nightmare.

But what of the few in whom the real killer instinct had been fostered and aroused? How do we sense it? How do we curtail it?

General Donovan had posed the questions to the psychologists and psychiatrists within OSS. Then he set them to work on a program to de-activate these human time-bombs. A program was set up to screen the returning agents, to release those who were already in a path of adjustment and to attempt to let the others down easily into civilian life. It all went into the discard with the sudden disbanding of the organization.

That worried him. It was something of vital importance left unfinished and there was nothing further he could do about it. But, as he so often said, it involved people and their lives. Those were the responsibilities he felt had been neglected under impersonal government action.

With characteristic directness he made every attempt to follow through personally. If, as an organization, OSS had failed in some respect to insure the future of its personnel, then he would do whatever was in his power to help. During the entire war he had been in close touch with his personnel, aware of their personal problems whether they might be financial, family or marital. Always he had been available to every man and woman for counsel. It was the trait which had won him such loyalty. It was still with him.

Now, from Sutton Place, he kept close personal contact with countless men and women who had been former associates in OSS. No problem was too personal, nothing was too trivial for him to handle so long as he could help. And with his infinite Irish charm the extent to which he could help was far-reaching.

Entry into America and the chance of a new life for a former agent? General Donovan arranged it and saw that the matter was properly expedited and the individual established. Help for a family left by an agent killed on mission? He followed the program established by OSS for such cases and assured the future economic security of the persons involved. There was hospitalization and psychiatric treatment for those who had broken under the strain of Nazi tortures but had miraculously lived through them. General Donovan followed that program closely and with keen eagerness to reestablish normal life patterns for those who could be rehabilitated.

The occasional personal tragedy of a former OSS operative concerned him deeply.

There was the case of the young officer who had had a brilliant record within the organization. He had served with distinction throughout the war. He had been cool, stable, decisive under the most perilous conditions. He had returned to Washington, he had been decorated for bravery and he had been demobilized. Our screening psychologists and psychiatrists had marked him high in adjustment. There would be no problem, so they said, in his return to the normal patterns of civilian life.

Certainly his future indicated an upward curve. He had an attractive wife, small children and a pleasant house in the country. His career was advancing well; there were no financial difficulties of any kind. It was a pleasant, happy existence.

Then, quite calmly one evening as he was sitting before the fire with his wife, he put aside his newspaper and stared for silent minutes into the flames. And when he broke the silence it was to state, quite calmly and without emotion, that he felt sometimes as if he were losing his mind. His wife thought it a joke. She laughed at him and passed it off. The idea was too preposterous to take seriously.

A couple of weeks went by. Then again, just as casually, he made a similar reference to his condition. And again his wife chided him for such morbid thoughts. She pointed out to him the foolishness of such a statement, that no one could be more normal. She dismissed the matter.

Three days later he took a revolver out of the desk in his office and blew out his brains.

To General Donovan this young officer was a war casualty of the most distressing kind. He should not have been a casualty at all. And on the surface he wasn't. Yet something deep down, something no one could get at, had lurked there within to destroy him. Whether it was the nightmare of an agent lost, a mission aborted, or some inner self-criticism or blame, no one will ever know; but whatever it was it had worked on this young officer until it had defeated him.

The fact that OSS had not been able to prevent it was a mark of failure in the General's opinion. We had sought to avoid this type of tragedy, the delayed action shock that could take a man's life; but somewhere the key had been lost. The fact that it might have been prevented haunted General Donovan as though it were through some personal failing of his own.

There was the young French girl who had been an agent. She had been successful, had supplied us with much information of value; and then the Gestapo had captured her with knowledge that she was spying for our services. She had been subjected to the most inhumane and bestial tortures in an effort to make her talk; but the tortures were terminated for the Nazis by the onrush of defeat. She was found alive and brought back to England for treatment.

Then, while the best available medical and mental experts

worked to help her, they had to stand by and watch her slip gradually into mental chaos. In spite of everything she became hopelessly insane, fated to spend the rest of her life in an institution.

Or the young officer who had mounted several highly successful missions behind enemy lines. He had worked long, nerve-snapping hours back-stopping his agent teams, supplying them and drawing the much desired information from them. Then, quite quietly one day after news had come through that one of his men had been lost, he just went on sitting at his desk, staring at the papers before him, not moving, not speaking, just sitting there.

He was finally persuaded to leave his desk and was led away, still in his trance, still shut off from the world as he had known it. The war was over for him. And he was finished as a man.

There was the occasional alcoholic who had taken to the bottle in an effort to erase the horrors of some particularly terrifying experience. And sadder still, for it was a kind of living murder, there were a few cases of agents who, having been prisoners of the Gestapo, had diabolically been made into drug addicts. Whether this latter cruelty had been the deliberate pattern of some Nazi sadist or whether it was the result of some of the so-called "medical experiments" of the torture camps no one will ever know. We only know that through the use of these drugs young men and women of character and ability were reduced to living shells of torment. To see them was to realize that the really lucky prisoners of the Gestapo were the dead ones.

And yet the fact that postwar breakdowns were relatively rare among returning OSS personnel spoke well for the rigorous training that had been provided. The careful screening, the pressure testing, the almost unendurable physical, mental and emotional stresses that had been deliberately built up in our training schools had, for the most part, eliminated the weak. Those who broke later were those who had endured terrors,

202

stresses and tortures beyond the wildest imaginings of any normal human.

The day he told me of Adrienne's suicide General Donovan was again disturbed by the failure of OSS to control such collapses.

"Why, when she had endured and survived so much, could we not have helped her to survive her own tortures?" he asked. And then he went on to say that he could never forgive himself for having given in to her persistent pleas to act as an agent. As if he thought he could make it all un-happen, he stated that only two or three of us knew the full horror of Adrienne's story and he wished never to discuss it again.

We never did.

But they were not all sad, those long discussions at Sutton Place. They were filled with pride and admiration for the hundreds of dedicated and courageous young men and women who kept the outfit going. And they were filled with laughter and wry amusement at the suddenly ridiculous or incongruous episode in the midst of the whole serious business of war.

He enjoyed finding courage and daring in unexpected places. It filled him with pride to discuss the fact that many men risked their lives quietly in some remote area far from the war zone in order to test a new weapon or discover a more efficient way of performing some specific operation. The young daredevil who endlessly tried flying a glider loaded with a jeep because he thought the Jeds or OGs could function better so equipped rated high marks in the General's esteem. The young officer who never left the United States and yet gave his life in an effort to perfect an ingenious sabotage weapon was as heroic as any agent and as important.

He still chuckled over the, to him, wonderful moment when I, expecting a messenger, had opened the door with a curt, "It's about time," only to discover one of Britain's highest ranking military men come to call. He never ceased to delight in going over the whole ridiculous story of our courier with the newsprint on her bottom. And he always was amused by the story of the highly efficient drop that was aimed at aiding the allied advance when the Germans were well on the run in retreat. Our team was dispatched, dropped in the dark of the moon and landed ready to go. They were somewhat chagrined to discover that our ground forces had advanced so fast in pursuit of the enemy our agents had landed in an Allied motor pool well back from the front. Yet General Donovan was quick to point out that there was still heroism there for the men had parachuted in good faith for a dangerous mission. It was only the fluid situation at the front that had made their assignment an amusing incident.

There was hardly ever a passing reference to the "prima donnas" who had appeared within the organization throughout the war. Most of them he dismissed with thinly veiled contempt. Yet, realist that he was, he gave credit for whatever they may have accomplished though he may have criticized the manner in which they operated. As long as the results were worthwhile he was ready to forgive much.

The complications, the hazards and the scope of agent financing never ceased to fascinate him. Many of the most exciting and certainly the most secret of all OSS operations involved the financing, and the General enjoyed recalling them and discussing them. Such fantasies as the liberation of a huge cache of enemy funds, so vast we weighed it rather than counted it, delighted him as did our ability to use the money against the enemy with success. And he was prideful of the fact that we had been so forehanded with our advance planning that OSS was able to furnish additional funds to invasion forces going in on D-Day at the request of the Army. Ours was the largest fund of safe French currency under a single control in the whole Allied operation.

The story of the vaults of the Bank of England being opened late one night to produce for OSS a scarce foreign gold currency pleased him on two counts. He was fascinated and proud to recognize that we could accomplish the apparently impossible under the most trying conditions. And, as an example of the immediate and full cooperation between the British and American services, it bore out his hard-hammered statements that such cooperation was not only necessary but possible. On it the outcome of the war depended. The fact that it was all accomplished by a couple of polite phone calls spoke volumes for British trust, organization and efficiency.

With the German surrender in May, 1945, the whole focus of OSS operation within the ETO was changed. Obviously the pressing need for agent teams no longer existed. But with the new problems presented by the German collapse the emphasis was shifted to so-called "situation reports." OSS had them. From the vast complex of Research and Analysis came the background material on the social, economic, political and ethnic problems to be considered in the rebuilding of Europe.

The endless talks setting up the postwar world, the vast undertaking of the Nuremburg trials, the Potsdam conferences, for all of these and more OSS had background material of tremendous scope and value. And it was available, immediate and up-dated.

But while the organization still continued to function actively in the research field, there was the tremendous problem of closing down field installations, training areas and all of the huge complex of a productive espionage and sabotage organization. Returning agents had to be de-activated. Hospitalization had to be arranged where necessary. The human factor in this great machine had to be considered. General Donovan turned it over to me.

Six months later I saw my way clear to leave the ETO. It was December of 1945 when I got back to Washington. General Donovan, long since a Major General, had left. Colonel Bruce was no longer with the organization. And Colonel Lane Rehm, who had so ably headed the Special Funds Branch of the OSS from Washington, had retired and named me in his place. It was now my job to pick up the loose ends of our agent financing throughout the world, close out the chains and provide for the carrying out of our obligations to the countless agents who had worked for the organization. The job was not made any easier by the constant high level shifting of command that was gradually chivvying OSS into non-existence.

General Donovan, in New York and during frequent trips to Washington, was still helpful. The immense problem of controlling the vast financial network of the OSS from Washington with a constantly diminishing staff was one he could appreciate. It was like an international banking house gone suddenly mad. A returning Far Eastern agent might turn up with a handful of yen, rupees, pounds and francs with a few guilders thrown in. Some might have been purchased in the open market at one rate, some through regular channels at an established rate. It was up to OSS Washington to reconcile the account and transfer it all to a dollar balance. The real nightmare was when an occasional agent returned with more money than he had originally been provided with because he had quite simply "liberated" some currency in the performance of his mission. It was unorthodox financing but it had been effective. From dollars we had strayed through pounds, francs (French, Belgian, Swiss and Algerian), guilders, kroner, marks, zlotys, pesetas, escudos, drachmas, rupees and yen and many others too numerous to list. There was gold of various nationalities, diamonds and occasional small items of high value such as jewelry and watches that were used as paying media. All had to be accounted for and reconciled for a final tally.

There were still obligations to agents and agents' families that had to be met. Many had arranged for long-range payments, some had asked for lump sum deposits in trust. These all had to be honored and credited. It was hardly surprising that the Army and Navy personnel newly brought into the

206

organization to facilitate its dissolution should have found it difficult to comprehend the situation. After all we had grown along with the operation, what had at first seemed unorthodox had now become commonplace, the unusual, the devious, the complex was boringly routine. It seemed strange to have to explain or to justify methods that practice had proven effective. General Donovan was of tremendous value and assistance in back-stopping much that had to be done.

It was April,1946.

The lights in the living room at Sutton Place were dim and soft and through the large windows of the room the panorama of the city sparkled over the East River. The bright gaiety of the world outside the windows made the whole four years just past seem unreal. It was almost as if they had not happened at all. For a moment I found myself wondering if this could have been true, if I had been a part of this nightmare world where the impossible was always possible, where simple, unexpected people had suddenly become self-effacing, unexpected heroes. Or perhaps I had just read some fantastic fable, a rather horrid *Through the Looking Glass*.

The General brought me out of it. He spoke of problems we had shared, of more people who had worked in OSS and his reminiscence went on, casually, quietly, almost as if he were talking to himself. It sounded slightly wistful, certainly nostalgic, as he told over again some of the deeds of high heroism, the acts of incredible daring and the plodding drudgery of fact-finding and reporting. It was a kind of summation of the OSS he had directed and known.

It was then I told him of my resignation from the OSS. The letter of resignation went in to the proper authorities on April 15, 1946. It requested my release from active duty within the organization to become effective on May 31, 1946. I outlined for him the work I had done since his own departure from OSS, the status of the affairs for which I had responsibility and the provisions made for a successor. I explained it all to him with emphasis on the reasons for the decision.

He listened to me in silence. His clear blue eyes were focussed steadily on me. His elbows rested on the arms of his chair, his fingertips were pressed against each other, and he gently flexed them again and again as I talked.

I must have sounded disillusioned. Certainly I had been critical. And I voiced dissatisfaction with the apparent lack of cohesion and efficiency within the fading organization which I was about to leave.

General Donovan looked at me piercingly. His voice was still the familiar soft, firm and warm voice I had so often found reassuring.

"War is strange, Bob. I shouldn't have to tell you that. It is everything that has ever been said about it and more. But mostly it is contradiction. It is order in chaos. It is efficiency in waste and vice versa. It is baseness and high valor. Cruelty and compassion."

He paused and his gaze shifted toward the high windows and out across the river with the blackness of the night and the sparkle of the light.

"Our particular kind of war, the kind of war OSS was forced to wage, may have been harder to take at times but I think that is only because you are closer to it. You see the trickery, the deceit, the treachery and the cunning close at hand and that's not pleasant. But then nothing is ever pleasant about war.

"But you also are closer to the good things, and there are good things in war. You see self-sacrificing on a scale you never had believed possible. You see self-effacement. Courage, bravery, resourcefulness, daring, plain guts, there just aren't words enough to cover the things you have seen some of our men and women do in the name of patriotism."

There was a long pause. Somewhere in the background

there was the slow, deliberate tick of a clock. All else was silence.

"You've seen it all," he went on, "and you are tired of it, as you should be. That's only natural. The war is over, long since. And with it has gone the zeal, the dedication and the spirit which helped us to win it. What you must do now, my boy, is to learn to live with the inconveniences of peace."

The inconveniences of peace! How right he was. For a full four years we had only to snap our fingers and a need was filled. All the money, all the supplies, all the weapons, all the ideas necessary to our aims had been supplied for the asking. The urgency of war had provided that. Now it was over.

I, for one, couldn't wait to embrace those inconveniences, whatever they might be.